LANGUAGE IN USE
INTERMEDIATE

SELF-STUDY
WORKBOOK
B

WITH ANSWER KEY

Adrian Doff
Christopher Jones

CAMBRIDGE
UNIVERSITY PRESS

Published by the Press Syndicate of the University of Cambridge
The Pitt Building, Trumpington Street, Cambridge CB2 1RP
40 West 20th Street, New York, NY 10011–4211, USA
10 Stamford Road, Oakleigh, Melbourne 3166, Australia

© Cambridge University Press 1994

First published 1994

Printed in Great Britain at the University Press, Cambridge.

ISBN 0 521 43555 2 Self-study Workbook
ISBN 0 521 43554 4 Self-study Workbook with Answer Key
ISBN 0 521 43552 8 Classroom Book
ISBN 0 521 43553 6 Teacher's Book
ISBN 0 521 43560 9 Class Cassette Set
ISBN 0 521 43561 7 Self-study Cassette Set

Split editions:
ISBN 0 521 43557 9 Self-study Workbook B with Answer Key
ISBN 0 521 43556 0 Self-study Workbook A with Answer Key
ISBN 0 521 43562 5 Self-study Cassette A
ISBN 0 521 43563 3 Self-study Cassette B
ISBN 0 521 43558 7 Classroom Book A
ISBN 0 521 43559 5 Classroom Book B

Contents

To the student

This Workbook contains exercises for you to do on your own.

Each Workbook unit begins with grammar or vocabulary exercises, which give extra practice in the language you have learned in class.

In addition, there are self-study exercises which help you to develop particular skills in English. These are:
- Listening skills (in each unit)
- Reading skills (in each Grammar unit)
- Writing skills (in each Vocabulary unit)
- Pronunciation (in Grammar units)
- Phrasal verbs (in Vocabulary units)

After every six units, there is a Review test.

There are also two Self-study Cassettes that go with the Workbook. You will need to use these for the Listening and Pronunciation exercises, some of the Phrasal verbs exercises, and the Dictation exercises in the Review tests.

Here is a short description of the exercises in the Workbook:

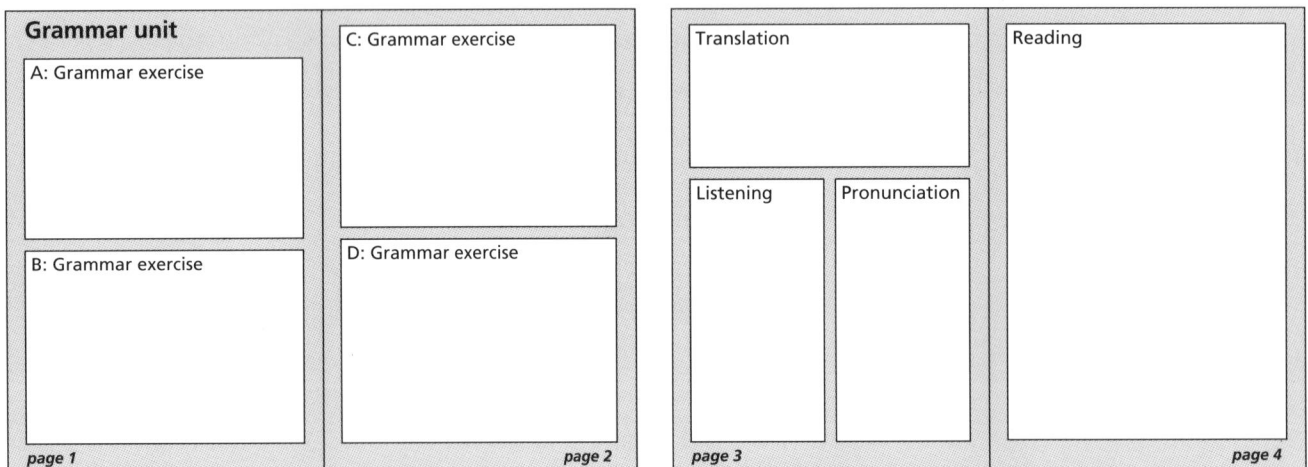

Grammar unit	
A: Grammar exercise	C: Grammar exercise
B: Grammar exercise	D: Grammar exercise
page 1	*page 2*

Translation	Reading
Listening	Pronunciation	
page 3	*page 4*

Grammar exercises
The grammar exercises give practice in the main structures of the unit. They usually include one puzzle or word game, and sometimes one freer exercise. There are three or four grammar exercises in each unit.

Translation
This section contains sentences for you to translate into your own language – and then back into English.

🔲 Listening
These are short listening tasks, which give you a chance to listen to natural English in your own time. Usually these are similar to one of the activities from the Classroom Book.

🔲 Pronunciation
These exercises give practice in pronunciation, stress and intonation.

Reading
This section contains reading tasks based on a variety of short texts. These include magazine and newspaper articles, letters, games and stories.

Vocabulary unit			Translation		Writing skills
A: Vocabulary exercise	C: Vocabulary exercise				
			Listening	Phrasal verbs	
B: Vocabulary exercise	New words				
page 1	*page 2*		*page 3*		*page 4*

Vocabulary exercises

The vocabulary exercises give practice in the main vocabulary areas of the unit. They usually include one puzzle or word game, and sometimes one freer exercise. There are two or three vocabulary exercises in each unit.

New words

This is a space for you to write down new words from the unit, together with your own notes and examples.

Translation

This section contains sentences for you to translate into your own language – and then back into English.

Listening

These are short listening tasks, which give you a chance to listen to natural English in your own time. Usually these are similar to one of the activities from the Classroom Book.

Phrasal verbs

These exercises teach a range of common phrasal verbs. You will sometimes need the cassette.

Writing skills

These exercises teach intermediate level writing skills, which include punctuation, using pronouns, joining sentences and organising ideas.

Guide to units

Self-study Workbook	Classroom Book
13 Comparing and evaluating	
Grammar exercises Listening: *Living in Britain* Pronunciation: *Linking words: consonant + consonant* Reading: *Left-handedness*	Comparing things; comparing the way people do things; criticising and complaining **Grammar:** comparative adjectives and adverbs; (not) as ... as ...; too & enough
14 The media	
Vocabulary exercises Listening: *Media habits* Phrasal verbs: *Double meanings* Writing skills: *Similarities*	**Vocabulary:** newspapers and magazines, and their contents; types of TV programme **Reading and listening activity:** *Easy listening*
15 Recent events	
Grammar exercises Listening: *What has happened?* Pronunciation: *Changing stress* Reading: *Personal letters*	Announcing news; giving and asking about details; talking about recent activities **Grammar:** Present perfect simple active & passive; Past simple; Present perfect continuous
16 Teaching and learning	
Vocabulary exercises Listening: *Three school subjects* Phrasal verbs: *Prepositional verbs (1)* Writing skills: *Letter writing*	**Vocabulary:** learning things at school; skills and abilities; education systems **Reading and listening activity:** *Improve your memory*
17 Narration	
Grammar exercises Listening: *Locked in!* Pronunciation: *Linking words with /w/ or /j/* Reading: *Strange – but true?*	Flashbacks in narration; changes in the past; reported speech and thought **Grammar:** Past perfect tense; reported speech structures
18 Breaking the law	
Vocabulary exercises Listening: *A case of fraud* Phrasal verbs: *Prepositional verbs (2)* Writing skills: *Defining and non-defining relative clauses*	**Vocabulary:** types of crime; types of punishment; courts and trials **Reading and listening activity:** *Detective Shadow*
Review Units 13–18	

Self-study Workbook	Classroom Book

19 Up to now

Grammar exercises Listening: *Favourite things* Pronunciation: *Stress and suffixes* Reading: *Four logic puzzles*	Saying when things started; saying how long things have (or haven't) been going on **Grammar:** Present perfect simple/continuous + for/since; negative duration structures

20 In your lifetime

Vocabulary exercises Listening: *Birth and marriage* Phrasal verbs: *Three-word verbs (1)* Writing skills: *Joining ideas: showing what's coming next*	**Vocabulary:** birth, marriage and death; age groups; age and the law **Reading and listening activity:** *A Good Boy, Griffith*

21 Finding out

Grammar exercises Listening: *Phone conversation* Pronunciation: *Changing tones* Reading: *A bit of luck*	Asking for information; reporting questions; checking **Grammar:** information questions; indirect questions; reported questions; question tags

22 Speaking personally

Vocabulary exercises Listening: *James Bond films* Phrasal verbs: *Three-word verbs (2)* Writing skills: *Sequence: unexpected events*	**Vocabulary:** ways of describing feelings; positive & negative reactions **Reading and listening activity:** *What's in a smile*

23 The unreal past

Grammar exercises Listening: *A better place* Pronunciation: *Common suffixes* Reading: *If things had been different …*	Imagining what would have happened in different circumstances; expressing regret **Grammar:** would have done; 2nd and 3rd conditionals; I wish + Past perfect; should(n't) have done

24 Life on Earth

Vocabulary exercises Listening: *How green are you?* Phrasal verbs: *Review* Writing skills: *Organising ideas*	**Vocabulary:** environmental problems and solutions; endangered species **Reading and listening activity:** *The Doomsday Asteroid*

Review Units 19–24

13 Comparing and evaluating

A Small and big differences

Write sentences that mean the same as the words in *italics*.

Example:
He's better-looking than I am, but *I'm much more intelligent.*
He isn't *nearly as intelligent as I am.*

Small differences		
Mary's	slightly a bit	taller (than John).
John isn't quite as tall (as Mary).		

Big differences		
Mary's	much far	more interesting (than John).
John isn't nearly as interesting (as Mary).		

1 Cars aren't as much fun as motorbikes, but *motorbikes are far more dangerous.*

   Cars aren't ....

2 CDs sound better than cassettes, but *cassettes aren't quite as expensive.*

   CDs are ....

3 *Greek isn't nearly as useful as English*, but it's a very beautiful language.

   English is ....

4 German mustard tastes very similar to French mustard, but *German mustard is slightly hotter.*

   French mustard isn't ....

5 *The bus takes a bit longer than the train*, but it's a lot cheaper.

   The train doesn't ....

6 I don't see why he got the job instead of me. *My qualifications are far better than his.*

   His qualifications aren't ....

B Comparison of adjectives and adverbs

Which of these words are adjectives and which are adverbs? Which could be either? Write *Adj*, *Adv* or *AA*.

good	fast
well	clearly
friendly	comfortable
hard	funny

Adjectives ...

He's a **fluent** speaker. → He's a **more fluent** speaker than I am.
She's a **hard** worker. → She's a **harder** worker than I am.

... and adverbs

He speaks **fluently**. → He speaks **more fluently** than I do.
She works **hard**. → She works **harder** than I do.

Now fill the gaps in these sentences with comparative forms of the words in the box.

1 You're a .... cook than I am. Why don't you cook lunch?

2 You're playing .... than you were a few months ago.

3 Our new neighbours are .... than the old ones.

4 We'll all have to try a bit ....

5 She can run .... than anyone else in the school.

6 I can see much .... with these new glasses.

7 Why don't you sit in this chair. You'd be much ....

8 Don't you know any .... jokes than that?

C Too and enough

Tom had a bad time last week. Here are some of the things that happened to him. Write two sentences about each one, using *too* and *enough*. Use the words in brackets in your answers.

Example: He wanted a £7,000 car, but he only had £5,000.

The car was too expensive. (expensive)
He didn't have enough money (to buy it). (money)

Too and enough
They've got **too** many children.
They haven't got **enough** bedrooms.
Their flat is **too** small.
isn't big **enough**.
They're **too** poor
They're not rich **enough** } to move house.

1 He sat on a chair and it broke under his weight.

.... (heavy)

.... (strong)

2 He received a letter written in Spanish, and he could only understand a bit of it.

.... (difficult)

.... (good)

3 He tried to climb a mountain, but half way up he had to give up.

.... (high)

.... (fit)

4 He did an exam with 20 questions, but he only had time to do 15 of them.

.... (questions)

.... (time)

D I'd rather ...

Look at the example, and write a similar answer to one of the questions below.

Example: Would you rather have a car or a motorbike?

Motorbikes cost less than cars, and they're cheaper to run. They're also faster. On the other hand, they're much more dangerous than cars, and they're not very pleasant to ride in bad weather. And you can carry more people in a car, and a lot more luggage. So on the whole I'd rather have a car.

Would you rather ...

... have a word-processor or a typewriter?
... live in Britain or the USA?
... have a TV or a radio?
... go camping or stay in a hotel?
... cook a meal or wash the dishes?
... be a student or a teacher?
... be male or female?

....

....

....

....

....

....

....

TRANSLATION

Translate into your own language:

1 He works much harder than he used to.

....

....

2 Windsurfing's OK, but it isn't nearly as much fun as water-skiing.

....

....

....

3 Are you sure there's enough food for everyone?

....

....

Now cover up the left-hand side, and translate your sentences back into English.

LISTENING: Living in Britain

1 You will hear people from Poland, France and New Zealand saying what they find strange about living in Britain.

Here are some of the things they say. Before you listen, find pairs of expressions that you think go together (e.g. *separate taps* – *wash your hands*).

separate taps	people stared
cross the street	change gears
bump into someone	wash your hands
left-hand-side driving	seeing the car coming
walking in my shorts	'Oh I'm really sorry'

[cassette] Now listen and check your answers.

2 [cassette] Listen again and answer the questions.

Speaker 1
a Why does she find separate taps a problem?
b Why can't she change gears?
c How does she feel when she crosses the street?

Speaker 2
a What are English people like?
b How do they behave in queues?

Speaker 3
a What was he wearing?
b What wasn't he wearing?
c Why did people stare?

PRONUNCIATION: Linking words: consonant + consonant

1 [cassette] Listen to these pairs of words. The first ends in a consonant sound, and the second begins with a consonant sound. Notice how they are linked together.

big girl	sit down	Government troops
red dog	take back	electric drill
phone bill	good boy	food processor
credit card	fast train	village square
desk top	art gallery	carving knife

2 Find links between words ending and beginning in a consonant sound in these sentences. Draw lines to connect them.

a Is it good luck to see a black cat?

b The next train to Prague goes in ten minutes.

c The clock said ten past two.

d I bought two bedside tables and some red curtains.

e We had fish soup and French bread.

f Like most people, I sometimes feel lonely.

[cassette] Now listen and practise saying the sentences.

READING: Left-handedness

1 **Before you read, look at these statements. Do you think they are true or false?**

a Most Chinese people are right-handed.

b Most Siamese twins are left-handed.

c On average, left-handed children are slightly more intelligent than right-handed children.

d The word for 'left' in most languages has a negative meaning.

e Japanese macaque monkeys are more likely to be right-pawed than left-pawed.

f The US army is more likely to accept you if you're left-handed than if you're right-handed.

g Most right-handed people are also right-footed.

h The text and pictures are the work of a left-handed person.

Now check your answers in the text.

2 **How can you tell whether an elephant is right-tusked or left-tusked?**

3 **Why do left-handed players have an advantage in tennis?**

4 **Here are some possible reasons why most people are right-handed. Which two agree with the text?**

a Left-handed people aren't very good at using tools.

b Early tools had to be shared.

c Right arms are stronger than left arms.

d Left arms are stronger than right arms.

e Babies copy their mothers.

f Babies like to feel their mother's heartbeat.

5 **Are you right-eyed or left-eyed?**

LEFT-HANDEDNESS
BY HUNKIN

LANGUAGE
MOST LANGUAGES ARE BIASED AGAINST LEFT-HANDERS:

ENGLISH: RIGHT (CORRECT)   LEFT (LEFT OUT)

FRENCH: DROIT (ADROIT)   GAUCHE

LATIN: DEXTER (DEXTROUS)   SINISTER

GREEK: IS AN EXCEPTION. ARISTEROS (LEFT-HANDED) ALSO MEANS BETTER

INTERNATIONAL
THE ESKIMOS, MAORIS, AFRICANS & CHINESE ARE ALL PREDOMINANTLY RIGHT-HANDED. SO WERE THE ANCIENT EGYPTIANS, GREEKS & ROMANS.

ELEPHANTS
AFRICAN ELEPHANTS ARE LEFT- OR RIGHT-TUSKED. ONE TUSK IS USED FOR DIGGING & IS SLIGHTLY LARGER THAN THE OTHER.

WHY MAN DEVELOPED A RIGHT-HAND BIAS

THEORY 1
WHEN ONE-HAND-SIDED TOOLS, SUCH AS SCYTHES & SICKLES, FIRST APPEARED, THEY WERE PRECIOUS OBJECTS OWNED BY THE COMMUNITY - NOT BY INDIVIDUALS. IT WAS OBVIOUSLY DESIRABLE THAT EVERYBODY SHOULD BE ABLE TO USE THE SAME TOOLS - SO A ONE-HAND-SIDED BIAS DEVELOPED.

THEORY 2
IT MAY BE INSTINCTIVE FOR WOMEN TO CRADLE BABIES ON THEIR LEFT SIDE - NEXT TO THE HEARTBEAT. THIS LEAVES ONLY THE RIGHT HAND FREE TO DO THINGS.

SIAMESE TWINS
SIAMESE TWINS ARE MIRROR IMAGES OF EACH OTHER. ONE WILL BE LEFT-HANDED & THE OTHER RIGHT-HANDED. THE FINGERPRINTS OF ONE TWIN'S RIGHT HAND WILL BE ALMOST IDENTICAL TO THE OTHER TWIN'S LEFT HAND.

☆ THE US ARMY REJECTS A HIGHER PERCENTAGE OF LEFT-HANDERS THAN RIGHT-HANDERS.

☆ LEFT-HANDED US SCHOOLCHILDREN HAVE ON AVERAGE, SLIGHTLY HIGHER IQs.

☆ IN MENTAL INSTITUTIONS, MORE PEOPLE THAN AVERAGE ARE LEFT-HANDED.

☆ HUNKIN IS LEFT-HANDED.

MONKEYS
A RECENT STUDY OF JAPANESE MACAQUE MONKEYS REVEALED:
40% LEFT-PAWED
20% RIGHT-PAWED
40% AMBIDEXTROUS

FEET
MOST RIGHT-HANDED FOOTBALLERS PREFER TO USE THEIR LEFT FOOT.

HOW TO FIND IF YOU ARE LEFT-EYED
FOCUS EYES ON DISTANT OBJECT. RAISE FINGER SO YOU SEE IT 'OUT OF FOCUS', IN FRONT OF OBJECT. WINK ONE EYE THEN THE OTHER. FINGER WILL APPEAR TO JUMP WHEN YOU WINK DOMINANT EYE BUT NOT THE OTHER.

SPORT
IN MANY SPORTS, SUCH AS CRICKET, TENNIS & FENCING, IT IS AN ADVANTAGE TO BE LEFT-HANDED. LEFT-HANDED PLAYERS GET USED TO RIGHT-HANDED OPPONENTS, BUT RIGHT-HANDED PLAYERS ARE OFTEN CONFUSED BY A LEFT-HANDED OPPONENT.

MOST RIGHT-HANDERS ARE RIGHT-EYED. THERE IS SOME EVIDENCE THAT THEY ALSO CHEW MORE WITH THE RIGHT SIDE OF THE JAW.

From *Almost Everything There is to Know*, by Hunkin, published by Hamlyn.

14 The media

A Which page?

On which page(s) would you expect to find these newspaper extracts? Write the page numbers in the spaces provided.

ON OTHER PAGES

Home news	2–5
International news	6–10
Financial news	11–12
Leading articles	13
Letters	14
Arts & Entertainment	15–16
Obituaries	17
Classified advertisements	17
Horoscope	18
Cartoons	18
TV and Radio	19–20
Sport	21–24
Weather	24
Crossword	24

1 page ...*17*....

After leaving university she joined a law firm, but her real love was politics, and at the age of 29 she became Labour Member of Parliament for

2 page ....

13 Farm animal (5)

3 page ....

Sir,
I am writing to complain about

4 page ....

A 10-year-old girl was in hospital last night after she

5 page ....

Capricorn
Although you could be having problems at work this week, your social life has never been better.

6 page ....

CHAMPIONS LOSE 2-1

7 page ....

Tonight temperatures will drop to around 3° in the north, but in the south they will stay around 8°. Rain

8 page ....

The US dollar dropped nearly 2 pfennigs against the German mark

9 page ....

8.00 That's Showbiz! *Boring chat show presented by Leonora*

10 page ....

American officials flew to Moscow yesterday for urgent discussions

11 page ....

FOR SALE 1992 Ford Escort 4-door

12 page ....

It is always a pleasure to hear Emily Baker sing in a title role, and last night's performance in *Carmen* was

13 page ....

This time the Government has gone too far. When will they realise that they were elected to serve the people

14 page .... ·

B TV programmes

Write about two programmes that you watch (or don't watch!) on TV. Say what kind of programme it is and what you like and don't like about it.

cartoon	crime series	news
chat show	documentary	soap
comedy	game show	sports

Example: *'That's Showbiz!' is a popular chat show. It has two or three film stars each week, and a singer or group. It's usually very boring, but sometimes one of the guests is quite interesting, and they often have good music.*

1 ....

....

....

....

2 ....

....

....

....

C Understanding the headlines

Read the information about newspaper headlines in the box. Then look at the headlines below and explain what they mean.

Headlines: a rough guide
The **Present simple** = someone **has done** something **UNEMPLOYED MAN WINS £1M** *means* An unemployed man has won a million pounds
The **Past participle** = something **has been done** **THREE KILLED IN HOUSE FIRE** *means* Three people have been killed in a house fire
The **infinitive** = something **is going to happen** **PM TO VISIT CHINA** *means* The Prime Minister is going to visit China

1
MONA LISA STOLEN

2
NEW SHAKESPEARE PLAY DISCOVERED

3
BANK MANAGER DISAPPEARS WITH £1M

4
12-YEAR-OLD CLIMBS EVEREST

5
ELECTRICITY PRICES TO RISE BY 150%

6
WHITE HOUSE DAMAGED BY BOMB

7
BRITAIN TO BECOME REPUBLIC ON JAN 1

8
CHIMPANZEE WINS CHESS GAME

1 ....
2 ....
3 ....
4 ....
5 ....
6 ....
7 ....
8 ....

New words

Use this space to write down new words from the unit, with your own notes and examples.

TRANSLATION

Translate into your own language:

1 I put an advertisement in the local paper, but no-one answered it.

....

....

2 – Is *Women Today* a monthly magazine?
   – No, it comes out once a fortnight.

....

....

....

3 – Is there anything good on TV tonight?
   – Yes. There's a documentary on after the news.

....

....

....

Now cover up the left-hand side, and translate your sentences back into English.

LISTENING: Media habits

1 ▭ You will hear two people talking about how they use the media. What do they read, watch and listen to? Listen and complete the tables.

Speaker 1	
Newspaper	
Magazines	
TV	
Radio	

Speaker 2	
Newspaper	
Magazines	
TV	
Radio	

2 Which speaker might say these things? (Write *1*, *2* or *Both*.)

   a 'I like to follow the news.'
   b 'I think television is rather a waste of time.'
   c 'I do the crossword every day.'
   d 'I love listening to the radio.'
   e 'I like to relax and watch a good thriller.'
   f 'I find science very interesting.'
   g 'I'm a lecturer in Business Studies in Edinburgh.'

PHRASAL VERBS: Double meanings

1 Each of the phrasal verbs can have two of the meanings given below. Match them, using a dictionary to help you.

   give away ....   *look up* ....

   turn down ....   *pick up* ....

   bring up ....   *put up* ....

   a have (s.o.) to stay   g collect, meet
   b reveal a secret   h make quieter
   c introduce a topic   i visit (after a long time)
   d take from the floor   j build, construct
   e give to other people   k try to find (in a book)
   f raise (a child)   l say 'no' to someone

2 ▭ Listen to the recording. Which meaning of the phrasal verb do you hear each time?

3 Complete these sentences using a phrasal verb.
   a He applied for promotion, but they ...
   b I don't know the French for 'tape recorder'. Why don't we ...
   c I don't need all these old clothes. I think I'll ...
   d We've got a spare room. We can ...
   e The radio's keeping me awake. Could you ...
   f He lives in Mexico City. If you're going there, why don't you ...
   g Just leave your suitcases at the school. I'm going that way, so I can ...
   h My parents died when I was a baby, so my grandparents ...

See also the Phrasal verbs reference section on the last page of the book.

WRITING SKILLS: Similarities

1 Look at these examples.

Tanya comes from a large family, *and so* does her husband.
Both Tanya and her husband ⎤
Tanya and her husband *both* ⎦ come from large families.

New York is a violent city, *and so* are Washington and Miami.
New York, Washington and Miami are *all* violent cities.

Compared with most countries, Norway *doesn't* have serious economic problems, *and nor* does Sweden.
Compared with most countries, *neither* Norway *nor* Sweden has serious economic problems.

2 Make sentences like those in the examples about

a tobacco and alcohol

....

b lions and wolves

....

c Tokyo, Hong Kong and Singapore

....

d Abraham Lincoln and John F Kennedy

....

3 Notice how we can develop the sentences in Part 1 into paragraphs.

Tanya and her husband both come from large families. *Both of them* have living grandparents and a large number of uncles, aunts and cousins.

New York, Washington and Miami are all violent cities. *In all three cities* there's a high crime rate and it's dangerous to walk in the streets at night.

Compared with most countries, neither Norway nor Sweden has serious economic problems. *Both countries* have small populations and plenty of natural resources.

4 Write similar paragraphs based on these notes.

a John/Richard – talented musicians. Good singing voices. Play several different instruments.

....
....
....
....
....

b Mars/Jupiter – not able to support life. Very cold. No oxygen in atmosphere.

....
....
....

c Christianity/Islam/Buddhism – major world religions. Have spread through many countries. Millions of followers. Influence on art and literature.

....
....
....
....

15 Recent events

A Personal news

Write paragraphs based on the notes in the boxes.

Example:

I've won £5,000 in the national lottery. The money arrived yesterday. I haven't decided how to spend it yet, but I'll probably buy a motorbike and go on a long holiday.

win £5,000 in national lottery
money arrive yesterday
not decide how to spend it
probably buy motorbike – go
on long holiday

1 ....

finally arrive in Turkey
get here yesterday
not very good trip – break down twice
find lovely little apartment by the sea
food good – sea warm
everyone very friendly

2 ....

give up smoking
two weeks ago
very difficult at first
now much easier
put on a lot of weight
never smoke again

Now write about a real piece of news about yourself.

3 ....

B Asking questions

Look at these news items, and ask questions based on the notes in the boxes. For each item, add a question of your own.

1 Thieves have broken into a bank and stolen £2,000,000.

Who did it?
....
....
....

> Someone did it. They got in somehow. Either they've been caught or they haven't.

2 A light plane has crashed.

....
....
....
....

> Something caused the crash. It happened somewhere. Either the people on board were killed or they weren't.

3 A manned spacecraft has landed on Mars.

....
....
....
....

> They arrived some time. It probably took a long time to get there. Maybe they've sent back some photos.

C What have they been doing?

Write sentences saying what these people *have been doing.*

Example: He's seen the news, a soap, and a movie.
He's been watching television.

> **Present perfect continuous**
>
> **have/has been + -ing**
> **I've been sitting** in the park.
> **She's been reading** a novel.

1 She's written to her grandmother, an old schoolfriend and her boyfriend.

....

2 They've polished the furniture, vacuumed the living room carpet and done the washing up.

....

3 He's done two workbook exercises, learned 10 irregular verbs and written a composition.

....

4 They've painted the bedroom ceiling and wallpapered the living room.

....

5 She's had a bath, changed her clothes and put on some make-up.

....

6 He's won one game of chess, drawn one game, and lost two games.

....

7 She's read the front page, the obituaries, and the sports news.

....

TRANSLATION

Translate into your own language:

1 They've won the election. I heard it on the news this afternoon.

....

....

2 – You look worn out.
  – I am a bit tired. I haven't been sleeping very well recently.

....

....

....

3 What's the matter with her? She's been behaving strangely all week.

....

....

....

Now cover up the left-hand side, and translate your sentences back into English.

LISTENING: What has happened?

1 Here are some key words from three telephone conversations. Which conversation do you think will be about

– a car breaking down?
– a party?
– a driving test?

a earrings – dolphin – dance – lounge – ring back

b relief – examiner – relaxed – reversing – celebration

c oil – battery – airport – borrow – insurance – favour

2 [cassette] Now listen to the conversations and answer the questions.

Conversation 1

– What has happened?
– How did the woman spend the evening?
– What is the man going to do?

Conversation 2

– How does the man feel?
  Why?
– Why does the woman say 'third time lucky'?
– What are they going to do?

Conversation 3

– What has happened?
– What does the woman want to do?
  Why?
– Is it the first time this has happened?
  How do we know?

PRONUNCIATION: Changing stress

1 [cassette] Listen to these two-line conversations. Notice how the stress changes in the replies.

– When shall we go?
– How about next week?

– I can't go this week.
– How about next week?

– Where's the suitcase?
– It's under the bed.

– Is it on the bed?
– It's under the bed.

2 Look at these conversations. Which words will be stressed in the replies? Underline them.

a – Let's get them a present.
  – I've bought some chocolates.

b – Shall we get some chocolates?
  – I've bought some chocolates.

c – I haven't seen you recently.
  – I've been on holiday.

d – When are you going on holiday?
  – I've been on holiday.

e – I'm thirsty.
  – Do you want some orange juice?

f – I don't like pineapple juice.
  – Do you want some orange juice?

[cassette] Now listen and practise saying the conversations.

READING: Personal letters

Here are parts of three letters to friends. The writers are Alan, Katrina and Jim.

Alan

I didn't realise there would be so much paperwork. First, you have to register with the police, and then there's the endless business of getting a resident's permit. I think I've spent half my time in the past month standing in queues! It must be terribly difficult for people who don't speak the language – it's really complicated and all of the forms are in German. Mine was pretty rusty when I arrived, but it's all coming back now.

Working hasn't been a problem. The 'office' is a spare bedroom containing one (old) word-processor and one (new) fax machine, which is all I need to keep in touch with the publishers back home.

The main difference about living here is that because it's much warmer, you're outside a lot more. For example, I've bought an old bike (new ones get stolen!) for getting around the city – I'm hardly using the car at all. And there are freshwater lakes nearby where the water's warm enough to swim in (they're good for sailing, too – but we haven't got a boat yet). Best of all, you're just up the road from the Alps. We've been quite a few times at the weekends: you take the cable car to the top of the mountain (where there's always a place you can have coffee!) and then walk down.

Katrina

You wouldn't believe the amount of stuff I've accumulated over the years. I've thrown away all the administrative papers, but have kept all the books and teaching materials — you never know, I might need them again. So there are now four crates and ten large boxes sitting in the front room. So I've got a great excuse if anyone asks me to do any work: I can't get across the room to my desk! It is cluttering the place up a bit, but it looks as if two of the children may be moving out over the next few months, so when that happens I'll just put it all into one of their rooms.

The best thing is that now I've actually got enough <u>time</u> to do what I want to do. Like lying in bed in the mornings, instead of jumping up and getting dressed at 7 o'clock. And doing a full 15 minutes of exercise every morning instead of the usual 3. And going into town in the afternoon and just wandering around and going into bookshops, and buying books that I <u>like</u> (rather than books that I need). And of course there's the theatre: I've been to three operas and two plays in the last two weeks alone. And it's great to have time at last to get in touch with old friends. It's so easy to lose touch.

Jim

The motorbike's great for getting around London in heavy traffic (though the insurance is incredibly expensive). I had a bit of a problem at first carrying the horn on the back, because it was wider than the bike, and I kept taking the wing mirrors off cars. So now I've had the horn cut in two, so I can carry it around in two bits and then screw it back together again when I arrive. It sounds just as good as it did before – to me at any rate.

Not much luck so far with the flat-hunting. All the places I like seem to be ridiculously expensive. Once you get further out towards Heathrow, there are some great places going quite cheap, but when you visit them you realise why – you can just about see the people waving from the planes as they go past. So I'm still looking.

Otherwise, there's not much going on. We don't finish till late most evenings, so the social life's suffering a bit. And there'll be no time – or money – to go on holiday this year. But as someone once said, 'Holidays are for people who don't like work.'

1 Choose an occupation for each of the writers.

actor	musician	teacher
bookseller	publisher	translator
climber	secretary	writer

2 According to the letters, who has/have …

a … recently moved?
b … recently retired?
c … been getting fit?
d … been looking for somewhere to live?
e … been working in the evenings?
f … been going out a lot in the evenings?

3 Mark these statements *T* (= true), *F* (= false) or *?* (= can't tell).

a Alan is German.
b Alan has rented an office to work in.
c Alan enjoys being in the open air.
d Katrina lives alone.
e Katrina is fond of reading.
f Katrina hasn't got enough space at home.
g Jim bought his motorbike second-hand.
h Jim wants to live near Heathrow Airport.
i Jim enjoys his work.

16 Teaching and learning

A School subjects

Look at the remarks in bubbles. What school subjects are the speakers talking about?
Write them in the diagram, and then complete the sentence in number 10.

1
I enjoy learning about how people used to live, but I can never remember all the dates.

2
We listen to a lot of symphonies, but we don't actually learn to play any instruments ourselves.

3
Arithmetic and geometry were OK, but now we're doing algebra it's a bit more difficult.

4
At the moment, we're doing *King Lear*, and *Anna Karenina*.

5
Most of the time, we just draw and paint.

6
Today we had a test on mountains and deserts.

7
We learn about animals and plants – all living things.

8
We all do French, but we can also choose Russian or Chinese.

9
Well the formula for water is H_2O, and that means two atoms of hydrogen and one of oxygen.

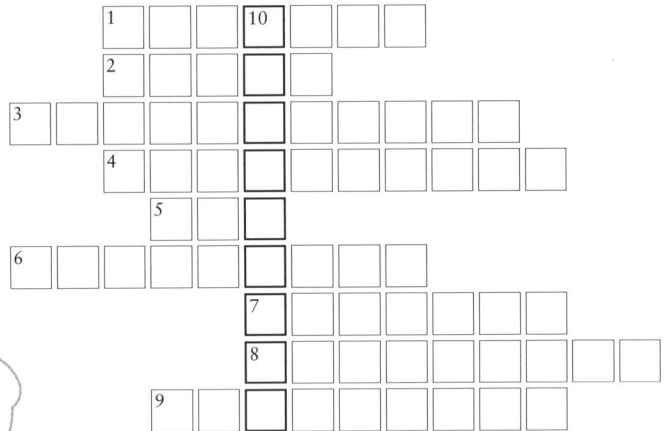

10 I have to study too many subjects. Just look at my ....!

B School report

Which school subjects are (or were) you good at, and not so good at? Why? Write about three subjects.

Ability			
I'm	no good not very good quite good very good	at	sports English taking exams learning dates

Examples:

I'm quite good at maths. I like working with numbers and I can work things out in my head without using a calculator.

I'm not very good at history. I can never remember dates, and I mix up all the names of the kings and queens and politicians and battles.

1 ....

....

....

2 ....

....

....

3 ....

....

....

C What's the system?

Write about the education system in your country, using the questions as a guide.

> At what age do children start primary school?

> When do they start secondary school?

> What different types of secondary school are there?

> What's the school leaving age?

> What are the most important school exams?

> Do most people get a job when they leave school or do they go on to university or college?

> How long does it take to get a university degree?

....

....

....

....

....

....

....

....

....

....

....

New words

Use this space to write down new words from the unit, with your own notes and examples.

TRANSLATION

Translate into your own language:

1 – Do you know how to type?
   – Yes, but I'm not very good at it.

....

....

2 You can only get a place at the
  secretarial college if you pass the
  entrance examination.

....

....

....

3 I'm a university graduate. I've got a
  degree in maths and physics.

....

....

....

Now cover up the left-hand side, and translate your sentences back into English.

LISTENING: Three school subjects

You will hear four people remembering subjects
they did at school. They talk about biology,
history and general science.

1 Here are some of the words they use. Which
  words do you think go with each subject?
  (Write *B*, *H* or *S*.)

☐ Latin names	☐ dates
☐ famous people	☐ battles
☐ equipment	☐ plants
☐ experiment	☐ emperors

🔲 **Now listen and check your answers.**

2 🔲 **Listen again. Which of these statements
  are closest to what the four people say?**

  a We spent all our time learning facts by
      heart.
  b We didn't learn much about real life.
  c We had to copy words from the blackboard.
  d The teacher made the subject seem real and
      interesting.
  e We did lots of practice.
  f We didn't have a chance to find things out
      for ourselves.

PHRASAL VERBS: Prepositional verbs (1)

1 The phrasal verbs in this exercise all have the form
  verb + *preposition*. These prepositions always come
  before a noun or pronoun.

  Example: *look after*
  I'll *look after* the children.
  I'll *look after* them. (not I'll look them after.)

2 Here are some common phrasal verbs with
  prepositions. Match them with their meanings.

look after	resemble
look into	collect, pick up
call for	find (by chance)
run into	meet (by chance)
come across	care for
take after	investigate
take to	like, be attracted to

3 The phrasal verbs in these sentences are mixed up.
  Change them so that they make better sense.

  a I didn't *look into* him – he wasn't very friendly.
  b I *called for* an interesting old travel guide in a
      second-hand bookshop yesterday.
  c He's got a dog, but he doesn't *run into* it very well.
  d The police are *coming across* the burglaries.
  e I *look after* my mother – we have the same eyes.
  f I'll *take to* you at 6.30. Make sure you're ready!
  g I *took after* an old friend of mine the other day.

*See also the Phrasal verbs reference section on the last
page of the book.*

WRITING SKILLS: Letter writing

1 Look at these openings to letters. Which person is

a selling something?
b applying for a job?
c enquiring about places to stay?
d writing to an old friend?
e replying to a friend's letter?

1
> Dear Sue,
> Many thanks for your letter – how nice to hear from you.

2
> Dear Mr Bailey,
> I saw your advertisement in the Nursing Times for staff nurses in Canada.

3
> Dear Richard,
> You may be surprised to get a letter from me after such a long time.

4
> Dear Sir/Madam,
> I'm writing to ask you for information about accommodation in Scotland.

5
> Dear Ms Howard,
> Thank you for your letter of 15th May, enclosing a cheque for £25.

2 Which of these sentences do you think continues each letter?

a I'm glad to hear that you're all well and that the children are fine.
b Unfortunately the jumper you ordered costs £30 including postage.
c I've been meaning to write for ages, but somehow I never quite got round to it.
d I'm thinking of staying there this summer, probably on the West coast.
e I would like to apply for the job, and enclose a curriculum vitae.

3 Now look at these endings. Which openings in Part 1 could they go with?

A
> I hope you'll be able to give me the information I need.
> Yours faithfully,

B
> Well, that's all for now.
> Hope to hear from you soon.
> Love,

C
> I look forward to hearing from you.
> Yours sincerely,

4 Choose one of these advertisements and write a letter. Use the examples above to help you.

BANANA T-SHIRTS

FOR   SALE

£15 each incl. postage.

Write to: T-Shirt Design, PO Box 54, Bristol BR2 2GD, England.

Luxury campsites in Northern Spain

For details write to:
Camping International,
25 Lombard Street,
London NW1A 2BR

WORK ON A YACHT THIS SUMMER

For details contact:
Bob Paterson, Cruise Crews, Box 153,
Kingston, Jamaica.

....
....
....
....
....
....
....
....
....
....
....
....
....
....
....

17 Narration

A What had happened?

Add a sentence to each item saying what *had happened*.

Example:

When I went down into the street, I couldn't find my car …

Someone had stolen it.
It had been stolen.

1 At the station, I jumped out of the taxi and ran onto the platform. But I was too late …

....

2 There was a man lying on the floor. As I got nearer I saw a neat round hole in the middle of his forehead …

....

3 I pushed the door, but it wouldn't open …

....

4 When I woke up, I found myself in a prison cell …

....

5 As soon as I got home, I went to get the diary from under the loose floorboard. It wasn't there …

....

6 When I showed the waitress a photo of Da Silva, she recognised it at once …

....

7 I smiled as Da Silva picked up the gun, pointed it at me and pulled the trigger. Nothing happened …

....

B Past states and previous actions

Write in the missing sentences.

	What were things like?	*What had happened?*
1	The coffee pot was empty.	*Someone had drunk all the coffee.*
2	*The window was broken.*	Someone had broken the window.
3	Her leg was bruised.	....
4	....	He'd washed his hands.
5	The light was on.	....
6	....	Someone had tidied the room.
7	It wasn't raining any more.	....
8	....	They had fallen asleep.

C Reported speech

Choose the most suitable speech bubble for each item, and complete the sentence using reported speech.

Actual words		Reported
does	→	did
is doing	→	was doing
can do	→	could do
will do	→	would do
did has done	→	had done

> You're going to have a fantastic week.

> I won't put up taxes.

> I've only just had dinner.

> I haven't finished it yet.

> You'll have to have an operation.

> We're doing all we can to solve the case.

> I missed the last bus.

> I don't want to see you any more.

1 I offered him something to eat, but he said that *he had only just had dinner.* .

2 In a TV interview, the President promised that ....

3 She got home at 2 a.m. and told her parents that ....

4 A police spokesman said that ....

5 She gave him back the ring and told him that ....

6 My horoscope was wrong, as usual. It said that ....

7 When I asked for my book back, he said that ....

8 I was horrified when the doctor told me that ....

D I realised …

Here are some scenes from stories in which people realised something. Write a short paragraph about each situation.

Example:

Jane was late. She arrived at the station just as the train was pulling out, and jumped on. Ten minutes later, the train stopped at a small station. Jane looked up from her book and read the name. Bottomley? Strange. They had never stopped there before. Then she realised that she was on the wrong train.

1 ....
....
....
....
....
....

2 ....
....
....
....
....

TRANSLATION

Translate into your own language:

1 I suddenly realised that I hadn't locked the door.

....

....

2 I hardly recognised him when I saw him a year later – he had changed so much.

....

....

....

3 She promised she'd get in touch as soon as she arrived.

....

....

Now cover up the left-hand side, and translate your sentences back into English.

LISTENING: Locked in!

1 🔲 You will hear someone talking about how he got stuck in an office in Madrid. Listen to Part 1 of the story and answer these questions.

   a Why didn't he notice that everyone had gone home?
   b Why couldn't he get out of the door?
   c Why couldn't he phone for help?
   d Why couldn't he climb out of a window?
   e Why did he want to get into the reception area?

2 Try to imagine how the story ends. Look at the outline below and fill the gaps.

He noticed a .... on the wall which

had lots of .... in it. By the light of

.... he managed to find a

.... for the .... On the

wall there was a list of ....,

including the .... He ....

him, and he came and ....

🔲 Now listen to Part 2 of the story, and check your answers.

PRONUNCIATION: Linking words with /w/ or /j/

1 🔲 When one word ends in a vowel sound and the next word begins with a vowel, we often add a /w/ or /j/ sound between them. Listen to these phrases:

Who‿are you?   Tea‿or coffee?
  /w/   /j/

No‿oranges   Fly‿away
  /w/   /j/

2 🔲 Which of these phrases will be linked with /w/ and which with /j/? Try saying them, then listen.

How interesting	Any others?
So am I	High up in the sky
My uncle	No overtaking
Two or more	Blue eyes

3 Find places in these sentences where words are linked with /w/ or /j/ sounds.

   a They all went to Amsterdam.
   b Who are you talking to on the phone?
   c Go up that way and you'll see it.
   d He isn't very easy to talk to.
   e How many are there? Three or four?

🔲 Now listen and practise saying the sentences.

READING: Strange – but true?

Australia

In July 1991, residents of the town of Victor Harbour complained that three whales were keeping them awake at night. The whales, which had arrived some days before, had got into the habit of falling asleep near the shore and snoring loudly.

Spain

In December 1990, a postman and his wife were injured when they opened a parcel that he had stolen from work and brought home. The parcel turned out to be a letter-bomb. The postman was later charged with theft.

Indonesia

In January 1991, police arrested a man for selling 'magic pencils' (£225 each) which he said would automatically produce correct answers in university entrance exams. According to the man, the pencils contained electronic signals which would confuse the computers marking the exams and correct wrong answers. Dozens of students complained that the magic hadn't worked for them.

Italy

In March 1990, an Italian American who had emigrated to the USA as a young man in 1948 flew to Italy for the first time in search of his only surviving relative – a great nephew whom he had never met. At his hotel in Rome, he got talking to the barman and explained why he had come – only to discover that the barman was his long-lost great nephew.

Poland

In May 1991, a candidate in a local Polish election decided to vote for his opponent out of politeness – and lost the seat. Out of 595 electors, he was the only one who had bothered to vote.

Great Britain

In August 1987, a Birmingham man was taken to hospital after trying to kill his wife. During the commercial break in a TV programme, he had gone out to the kitchen to make two coffees – one of them poisoned with arsenic. He had then got so involved in the programme (a crime show called *Inspector Morse*) that he had accidentally picked up the wrong cup and drunk it. He was charged with attempted murder.

USA

In 1971, a man went into a bank in Chicago to cash a blank stolen payroll cheque. The thief had made out the cheque to 'Miles F Huml', a name he had picked at random from the telephone directory. He handed the cheque to the bank clerk, who immediately sounded a silent alarm, and the man was arrested. The bank clerk's name was Mrs Miles F Huml. She said later 'I looked at the cheque and I looked at the man, and I knew he wasn't my husband.'

Bangladesh

In April 1991, a baby boy was swept away from a coastal village during a severe storm. He had been given up for dead when rescuers spotted a dolphin holding him in its mouth to keep him clear of the water. The dolphin allowed villagers to take the boy from its jaws. He was later treated for leg injuries caused by the dolphin's grip.

---

1 Here are some remarks that people might make about these eight stories. Which story (or stories) goes best with each one?

  a 'What an amazing coincidence!'
  b 'Extraordinary creatures, aren't they?'
  c 'Some people will believe anything.'
  d 'He got the punishment he deserved.'
  e 'Oh, that was really bad luck!'

2 Six of the stories appeared in newspapers. The other two were made up.
  Which two do you think were made up?

Answer to Question 2

The stories about Italy and Britain were made up. The others appeared in a variety of newspapers. Whether they are actually true, however, is not known.

Breaking the law

A Criminals and their crimes

What kind of criminals are these people? Find out by rearranging the letters of their names. Then imagine what each of them did and write a sentence about it.

1 Bob Err: *Robber*
   He robbed a bank in downtown New York, and got away with $250,000.
   ....

2 G Burral: ....
   ....
   ....

3 Rich Jake: ....
   ....
   ....

4 Reg Glums: ....
   ....
   ....

5 Clara Kimble: ....
   ....
   ....

6 R R Demure: ....
   ....
   ....

7 Phil Foster: ....
   ....
   ....

8 D V Alan: ....
   ....
   ....

9 Dan Kipper: ....
   ....
   ....

B Crime story

Fill the gaps in the text with words from the box.

On May 15, 1990, a masked gunman held up a London post office
and got away with £5,000. Two days later, Amanda Smith was
.... by police and .... with the crime.
Three months later, the .... began. The
.... claimed that Smith, who was unemployed, had spent
£3,000 on new clothes and household appliances on the day after the
robbery. They produced .... who said they had seen Smith
hanging around the post office for several days before the robbery took
place. The .... argued that there was not enough
........................., and added that Smith had been in Manchester visiting
her sister on the day of the robbery. The .... didn't take
long to make up their minds. After only 30 minutes they returned to
the court to deliver their ....: Smith was ....
The following day, the .... passed sentence: he imposed a
.... of £2,000 and sent Smith to .... for two
years. As she was led away from the ...., Smith shouted to
reporters 'They're wrong. I didn't do it. I'm ....!'

arrest	fine	prison
charge	guilty	prosecution
court	innocent	trial
defence	judge	verdict
evidence	jury	witnesses

New words

Use this space to write down new words from the unit, with your own notes and examples.

....

....

....

....

....

....

....

....

....

....

....

....

....

....

TRANSLATION

Translate into your own language:

1 They broke into the office and stole several secret documents.

....

....

2 They were arrested for drug smuggling and sentenced to ten years' imprisonment.

....

....

....

3 At the end of the trial, the jury found her 'Not guilty'.

....

....

Now cover up the left-hand side, and translate your sentences back into English.

LISTENING: A case of fraud

1 **You will hear about a man who thought of a clever way of making money. Before you listen, look these words up in a dictionary.**

fraud	generations	family tree
emigrate	greedy	make a fortune

2 [cassette] **Listen to Part 1, and complete what the man wrote in his letters.**

a
> Dear Mr Thomas,
>
> If you send us ...., we will find
>
> out your .... If we find that
>
> anyone in your .... was
>
> ...., we will send you your
>
> ....

b
> Dear Mr Thomas,
>
> We are sorry to have to tell you that
>
> there is .... in your
>
> ....

3 [cassette] **Listen to the second part and find five things that are different from this text:**

After a time, he became lazy and stopped sending letters. People in Canada started to complain. They investigated, but they never found the man. The speaker thinks it's a pity he wasn't caught.

PHRASAL VERBS: Prepositional verbs (2)

1 **Match these sentences with the the most suitable continuations in the box.**

a I *couldn't* possibly *do without* …

b I *could* really *do with* …

c The book *deals* mainly *with* …

d She's taking a long time to *get over* …

e They're finding it quite hard to *cope with* …

f Since my illness, I*'ve* really *gone off* …

> 1 … greasy food.
> 2 … her mother's death.
> 3 … my computer.
> 4 … bringing up five children.
> 5 … the Second World War.
> 6 … a long cold drink.

[cassette] **Now listen to the examples.**

2 **Replace the words in italics with phrasal verbs.**

a I really *stopped liking* children after my 5-year-old nephew came to stay.

b He just can't *handle* the pressure of his new job.

c The article *was about* new discoveries in physics.

d He had 'flu, but now he's *recovering from* it.

e I'*d like* someone to help in the office.

f I *really need* a cup of coffee in the morning.

See also the Phrasal verbs reference section on the last page of the book.

WRITING SKILLS: Defining and non-defining relative clauses

1 **Look at these pairs of sentences.**

A A friend of mine *who lives in Canada* is coming to stay next week.
B My cousin Peter, *who lives in Canada*, is coming to stay next week.

A What's the name of that novel *which became an international best-seller*?
B She wrote a novel called 'Gold', *which became an international best-seller*.

A She's going out with a man *(who) she met on holiday last year*.
B She's going out with a Hungarian called László, *who she met on holiday last year*.

A The place *where I grew up* is a typical seaside town.
B Bournemouth, *where I grew up*, is a typical seaside town.

The *A* sentences contain 'defining' relative clauses. They define what we are talking about (*Which friend?*, *Which novel?*, *Which man?*, *Which place?*). **There are** *no commas* **before or after the relative clause. Instead** of *who* or *which*, we could use *that*:

A friend of mine that lives in Canada is coming to stay next week.
What's the name of that novel that became an international best-seller?

The *B* **sentences contain 'non-defining' relative clauses. They just add more information. There are** *commas* **before (and after) the relative clause. We cannot use** *that* **instead of** *who* **or** *which*.

2 **Which of these are 'defining' and which are 'non-defining' relative clauses? Mark them** *D* **or** *ND*, **and add commas if necessary.**

a This is the lever which turns the engine on.
b This is my friend Sarah who I've known for more than 20 years.
c The people who live next door play loud music every evening.
d Is there a shop near here which sells bread?
e Sydney where I lived for ten years is a beautiful city.
f The first car that I ever drove was a Citroën 2CV.

3 **Join these ideas to make a paragraph of about seven sentences. Join the sentences with** *who, which, that, where* **or** *and*, **and add commas where necessary.**

I was sitting in a café. I often go there for a drink after work. I called the waiter. I know him quite well. I asked for a coffee and a ham sandwich. While I was waiting, I looked at a newspaper. It was lying on the table. I started reading an article on the front page. It said, 'Police are looking for a medical student, Veronica Hall. She has been missing from her home for two weeks.' I looked at the photograph. It showed a young woman with dark, curly hair. It was a face. I recognised it at once. She was my new next-door neighbour. She had moved in just two weeks before.

....
....
....
....
....
....
....
....
....
....
....
....
....
....

1 Sentence rewriting

Rewrite these sentences using the words given.

Example:

They deliver 300 million letters every day.

300 million letters *are delivered every day.*

1 My brother's slightly older than me.

I'm ....

2 You can't run nearly as fast as me.

I ....

3 The light switch is too high for my son to reach.

My son isn't ....

4 The police have recaptured an escaped prisoner.

An escaped prisoner ....

5 He's not a very good typist.

.... typing.

6 'They've already gone,' she thought to herself.

She realised that ....

7 The window was broken.

Someone ....

2 Verb forms

Write the correct form of the verbs.

Example:

His wallet *was stolen* (steal) while he was standing in a queue at the post office.

1 Now the news. Black's Hotel ....
(destroy) by fire. The fire ....
(start) in the kitchens last night and quickly
.... (spread) to other parts of the
building. Rescue workers ....
(*still* search) for two missing guests.

2 I .... (try) to lose weight recently.
I .... (give) up eating chips and
.... (do) a lot of exercise. So far
I .... (lose) nearly two kilos.

3 Susan was exhausted. She ....
(have) very little sleep the night before, and she
.... (*not* eat) anything all day.
Quietly, she .... (start) to cry.

3 Vocabulary

1 **Match the programmes with the descriptions.**

comedy show	gives you information
chat show	trying to win prizes
documentary	never-ending drama
game show	stars talking about themselves
soap	makes you laugh

2 **What school subject do you associate with**

a dates and battles? ....

b maps and climate? ....

c poetry and novels? ....

d doing calculations? ....

e doing experiments? ....

3 **Fill in the missing words.**

I started .... school when I was six,
and left .... school at 18. Then I went
to university and got a .... in languages.
So now I'm a university ....

4 **Write in the missing crimes or criminals.**

....	burglar
murder	....
....	blackmailer
vandalism	....
....	robber

5 **Match the items on the left with those on the right.**

the accused	give evidence
the defence	decide on the verdict
the judge	want a 'guilty' verdict
the jury	want a 'not guilty' verdict
the prosecution	the person on trial
the witnesses	the person in charge

4 Fill the gaps

Fill each gap with *one* suitable word. Example:

I ....*was*............ walking through the park yesterday when I suddenly ....*heard*............ a loud scream.

1 The first thing I do when I get my daily .... is to .... to the horoscope. Last
Tuesday, it .... me that I .... soon hear from some old friends. Sure enough, I
got a phone call from some friends from Australia. They .... just arrived at Heathrow
Airport, and said they would .... arriving at my house that evening.

2 I've always .... to learn to play the piano, so recently I've been .... lessons, and
I now know .... to read music. I'm not very good .... it yet, but I'm getting
.... all the time.

3 Last week I went into a local restaurant to .... lunch. It was terrible. They hadn't cooked the
chicken for long ...., and the chips had far too .... salt on them. When I
complained .... the waiter, he apologised and explained that he had .... the
meal himself, because the chef had .... taken to hospital suffering from food poisoning!

5 Writing paragraphs

Write a short paragraph (2 or 3 sentences) on the following:

1 Which do you prefer, travelling by car or travelling by train? Why?

....

....

....

2 What's your favourite newspaper or magazine? What do you like about it?

....

....

....

3 Think of a story that's in the news at the moment, and write a brief report for a radio news programme.

....

....

....

4 What do you think of the education system in your country? What's good and what's bad about it?

....

....

....

6 Dictation

You will hear a story about a charity shop which sells second-hand clothes.

Listen and write down what you hear.

19 Up to now

A Duration

1 Write out these sentences, choosing between the Present perfect simple and continuous, and between *for* and *since*.

Duration with since & for			
I've She's	been ill	for	six months two weeks
We've They've	known him been waiting	since	1990 September

  a I've *known/been knowing* them *for/since* more than 25 years.

  ....

  b He's *learned/been learning* Spanish *for/since* quite a long time.

  ....

  c We've only *had/been having* this video recorder *for/since* Saturday.

  ....

  d They've *played/been playing* cards *for/since* 9 o'clock this morning.

  ....

2 Now write similar sentences about the people in these newspaper clippings.

a

GARY AND EILEEN got engaged in July 1985, the day that Eileen left school – and they're still not married! 'We're not in any hurry,' said

b

HARRY PALMER had his first driving lesson on his 17th birthday. Yesterday he was 37, and he spent the morning having his 1205th driving lesson! Yes, Harry still hasn't

c

TOM KEMP had a piece of chewing gum in his mouth when he scored the winning goal in the Cup Final two years ago. He decided that it brought him luck, so he kept it – *and pops it into his mouth each time he plays!* 'I won't go onto the pitch without it,' says Tom,

d

LAST OCTOBER Ken Garret had an argument with his wife Janet over where they were going to spend Christmas. One thing led to another, and Ken ended up spending the night in the garage. *And he's still there!* 'I told him he couldn't come in until he apologised,' explains Janet, 'and he still hasn't. I wish he would, though. I miss him

  a ....

  b ....

  c ....

  d ....

3 Rewrite your last four answers using *since* + clause.

since + clause	
He's been ill (ever) since	he ate that chicken. he arrived. we went swimming.

  a ....

  ....

  b ....

  ....

  c ....

  ....

  d ....

B How long (ago) …?

Imagine that you're going to interview the people below. Ask questions with *How long …?* and *How long ago …?* Use the prompts for the first two people, and make up your own questions for the third.

Example: A novelist

How long ago did you decide to become a writer? (decide to become a writer)
How long have you been writing novels? (write novels)

1 A film star

.... (live in Beverly Hills)

.... (make your first film)

2 The President of IBM

.... (join the company)

.... (be President)

3 The lead guitarist of a band

....

....

C Negative duration

Write about three things that you haven't done for some time. Start by saying how long ago it was. The verbs in the box may give you some ideas.

buy	drink	go	play	see
clean	eat	lose	read	write

> **Three ways of expressing negative duration**
>
> I haven't had a decent meal for three days.
>
> It's a year since I (last) went to the theatre.
>
> The last time I rode a bike was | several years ago.
> | when I was a child.
> | in 1988.

Examples:

I haven't lost my glasses for at least six weeks. The last time was when I took them off to wash my face at a friend's house, and I left them there in the bathroom.

It's three years since I last went away for a holiday. These days I'm too busy to go away, and I can't afford it either.

The last time I drank sake was when I went to a Japanese restaurant last summer. I remember they served it warm. The meal was wonderful, but it was a bit expensive.

1 ....

....

....

2 ....

....

....

3 ....

....

....

TRANSLATION

Translate into your own language:

1 How long has Spain been a member of the European Community?

....

....

2 I've known her ever since she first came here five years ago.

....

....

3 It must be months since I last wrote a letter to anyone.

....

....

Now cover up the left-hand side, and translate your sentences back into English.

LISTENING: Favourite things

1 ▢ **You will hear three people talking about favourite possessions. Listen and decide which things in the pictures they are describing. Note down words the speakers use that helped.**

	Picture	Words
1		
2		
3		

a *b* *c*

d *e* *f*

2 ▢ **Listen again, and answer the questions.**

Speaker 1: When was the photo taken?
Who's in the picture?
Why does she like it?

Speaker 2: When and where did he buy the camera?
How did he get the money?

Speaker 3: When and where did he buy the gramophone?
Why does he like it?

PRONUNCIATION: Stress and suffixes

1 ▢ **Listen to these words on the tape. Notice how the main stress changes.**

invite	invitation
imagine	imagination
origin	original
photograph	photographic
national	nationality

2 **Look at the words in italics in these sentences. Where is the main stress?**

a He loves talking about *politics*.

There are two main *political* parties in Britain.

b We sold our *electric* cooker and bought a gas one.

Here's another bill from the *electricity* company.

c I don't know where he's gone – it's a *mystery*.

Her boyfriend is a rather *mysterious* person.

d The doctor *examined* my ears and nose.

The *examination* starts tomorrow.

e It tastes just like beer, but it contains no *alcohol*.

I'm afraid we don't serve *alcoholic* drinks.

▢ **Now listen and practise saying the words.**

READING: Four logic puzzles

1 Five people are waiting to see the doctor.

Sue came in ten minutes ago.
Richard has been waiting for half an hour – when he
  arrived, one person was already there.
Tom hasn't seen his friend Ursula for months, so he
  decided to sit next to her.
Ursula wanted the seat by the window, but it was
  already occupied.
Quentin broke his arm last week.

Whose turn is it to see the doctor?
What's wrong with Ursula?

2 Maria left school when she was 18, and spent four years at
  university.
She's been living in the USA ever since she left John.
John's three years older than Maria.
She hasn't seen John since his 30th birthday party.
It's eight years since Maria got her university degree.

How long has Maria been living in the USA?
How old is John?

3 The inhabitants of the island of Alithia always speak the truth. The inhabitants of the nearby island of Pseudia always lie. Here are some statements made by two married couples, one from each island.

Alice I'm married to Cecil.
     I've got two more children than Delia.
Brian I've got more than one child.
     I've been married for eight years.
Cecil I've been married for nine years.
     Brian got married a year before I did.
     He's got a son called Edgar.
Delia Alice is a liar.
     She's been married for longer than me.
     She's got four children.

Who is married to whom, and where do they live?
How long has each couple been married?
How many children does each couple have?

Alithia		Pseudia
	names?	
	years married?	
	how many children?	

4 Jim, Kate, Laura and Mike often play chess together at the weekends.
Can you complete the table, using the information below?

The teacher's been playing chess
  for two years.
The doctor's been playing for twice
  as long as Jim.
Jim taught the electrician to play a
  year ago.
Jim learned to play one year after
  the baker.
Kate always loses to the doctor, but
  she always beats Jim.
It's one week since the teacher had
  a game of chess.
In her last game, Laura beat the
  baker, who's a man.
Mike hasn't played since he lost to
  the doctor two weeks ago.

	Jim	Kate	Laura	Mike
What is his/her job?				
How long has he/she been playing?				
When did he/she last play?				
Against whom?				
Did he/she win or lose?				

20 In your lifetime

A ⬜⬜⬜⬜ ⬜⬜⬜⬜⬜ ⬜⬜ ⬜⬜⬜⬜⬜

Fill the gaps with words associated with birth, marriage and death. If your answers are right, the letters in circles will spell out the name of the exercise.

I arrived in the world very suddenly. Fortunately, our next door neighbour was a ⬜⬜⬜⬜⬜Ⓞ⬜ ,

and she rushed round to help with the ⬜⬜Ⓞ⬜⬜ . I was ⬜Ⓞ⬜⬜ on a Monday night, and my

Ⓞ⬜⬜⬜⬜ was back on her feet doing the housework by Wednesday morning. A few weeks later I

was Ⓞ⬜⬜⬜⬜⬜⬜⬜⬜ in the village church …

… In Britain, ⬜⬜Ⓞ⬜⬜⬜ traditionally wear long white dresses, and get ⬜Ⓞ⬜⬜⬜⬜⬜

in church. But my ⬜⬜⬜Ⓞ⬜⬜⬜⬜ was nothing like that. My husband-to-be was not a

⬜⬜Ⓞ⬜⬜⬜⬜⬜ man, and so the ceremony took place in a registry ⬜⬜⬜⬜Ⓞ .

Afterwards, we had a small ⬜⬜⬜⬜⬜Ⓞ⬜⬜ in the village hall, and went off on our

⬜⬜⬜⬜⬜Ⓞ⬜ : a weekend by the seaside …

… In my old ⬜⬜Ⓞ⬜ I often think about my own death. Should I be ⬜⬜⬜Ⓞ⬜⬜ in the

churchyard, or should I be ⬜⬜⬜⬜Ⓞ⬜⬜⬜ instead? Will I go to ⬜⬜⬜Ⓞ⬜⬜ after I

die, and what will it be like? And who will come to the ⬜⬜⬜Ⓞ⬜⬜ ?

B The time of your life

Choose two of the ages in the table, and say what is the best and worst thing about them.

Example:

The best thing about being a baby is that people do everything for you. The worst thing is that you can't talk, so you can't tell people what you want.

The	best / worst	thing about being	a baby / a child / a teenager / in your (20s) / middle-aged / elderly	is …

1 ....

....

....

....

....

2 ....

....

....

....

....

C What are they like?

Choose adjectives from the box which best describe these people. Use the pictures to help you.

shy	naughty	rebellious
wise	helpless	independent
lonely	ambitious	self-conscious

1 'He's always stealing sweets, and he pulls people's hair.' ....

2 'By the time she's 30, she wants to be a millionaire.' ....

3 'He knows a lot about the world, and people often ask him for his advice.' ....

4 'She doesn't know anyone – she's got no-one to talk to.' ....

5 'He thinks that everyone is looking at him all the time.' ....

6 'She manages very well without any help from us.' ....

7 'He's a bit scared of meeting new people.' ....

8 'She can't do anything herself – we do everything for her.' ....

9 'Whenever someone tells him what to do he argues about it.' ....

New words

Use this space to write down new words from the unit, with your own notes and examples.

TRANSLATION

Translate into your own language:

1 At a traditional wedding, the guests throw rice over the bride and groom.

....

....

....

2 He was quite shy as a teenager, but now he's become much more self-confident.

....

....

....

3 At what age are you allowed to vote in your country?

....

....

Now cover up the left-hand side, and translate your sentences back into English.

LISTENING: Birth and marriage

You will hear two stories. Story A is about having a baby. Story B is about a wedding.

1 Which of these words do you think will be in Story A and which in Story B, and which can't you be sure about? Mark them A, B or ?

trapeze act	Russians
pregnant	swimming pool
groom	circus tent
midwife	bride
clowns	hospital
pain	reception

🔲 **Now listen and check your answers.**

2 🔲 **Listen again and complete these sentences.**

Story A

a The woman decided to have a baby ...
b The advantage of this is that ...
c She managed to hire a ...
d She also found a good ...
e On May 11, 1985, she ...

Story B

f The man knew a couple who decided to ...
g They invited their friends to come ...
h At the reception, the couple ...
i They had spent a whole week ...

PHRASAL VERBS: Three-word verbs (1)

1 Some phrasal verbs have three parts: a verb, a particle and a preposition. Compare these sentences.

get on　　　I never visit my sister. We don't *get on*.
get on with　I don't *get on with* my sister.

2 Make three-word verbs by adding phrases from the box to these sentences.

a Your cough will only get better if you *cut down* ...
b I can't stop now – I must *get on* ...
c You can play in the street, but *look out* ...
d She walked quickly to *catch up* ...
e Could you go to the shop? We've *run out* ...

> 1　... *for* cars.　　　4　... *on* cigarettes.
> 2　... *with* the others.　5　... *with* my work.
> 3　... *of* sugar.

3 Fill each gap with a three-word verb.

a You go ahead. I'll .... you later.

b He's trying to .... meat and eat more vegetables.

c Could you .... the postman? I'm expecting a cheque.

d I don't want to go out. I'd rather stay here and .... my knitting.

e If we don't hurry, we'll .... time.

See also the Phrasal verbs reference section on the last page of the book.

WRITING SKILLS: Joining ideas: showing what's coming next

1 Look at these sentences. Find *one* suitable continuation for each of them in the box.

  a We arrived five minutes before the concert was due to begin. *Surprisingly* …

  b When I looked in my purse, I realised with a shock that I had no money to pay for the meal. *Fortunately* …

  c The room they gave me wasn't quite what I'd hoped for. It had a very small single bed, and there was nowhere to hang my clothes. *On the other hand* …

1 … most people were already sitting in their seats.	*4* … there was only a washbasin with a single cold tap.
2 … it was quiet, and I would be able to work without being disturbed.	*5* … there were still very few people in the auditorium.
3 … the waiter recognised me, and said I could bring in the money tomorrow.	*6* … the manager was very unfriendly, and insisted on taking my name and address.

2 Make sure that you understand the expressions in the box below. Use a dictionary if necessary. Then choose suitable expressions from the box to fill the gaps.

  a Terrorists planted a bomb at Istanbul Airport. ...., it was discovered before it exploded.

  b He entered the room wearing bright red silk pyjamas. ...., everyone stopped talking and stared at him.

  c At first, I didn't like the idea of eating boiled sea snake. ...., it tasted delicious.

  d Diesel vehicles don't have very good acceleration. ...., they're very economical to drive.

  e Pigs aren't as stupid as they look. ...., they're extremely intelligent.

  f I certainly didn't think the film was boring. ...., I really enjoyed it.

  g They were selling all their jackets at half-price. ...., there weren't any left in my size.

In fact
On the contrary
Surprisingly
Not surprisingly
Fortunately
Unfortunately
On the other hand

3 Write suitable continuations for these sentences:

  a She's certainly not lazy. On the contrary, ...
  ....

  b He went straight up to her and said 'Will you marry me?'. Not surprisingly, ...
  ....

  c Their car got stuck in a snowdrift. Fortunately, ...
  ....

  d The job isn't very well paid. On the other hand, ...
  ....

  e I was hoping to visit the Egyptian Museum while I was in Cairo. Unfortunately, ...
  ....

21 Finding out

A Questions

Write questions beginning *What* and *How*.

1 Has he got black hair? brown hair? blond hair?
What colour hair has he got?
....

2 Shall I wear a suit? jeans and a T-shirt? a jacket and tie?

....

3 Did it take you 10 minutes to find the house? 20 minutes? 30 minutes?

....

4 Do you use *Macleans* toothpaste? *Colgate*? *Crest*?

....

5 Do they visit the States every six months? every year? every two years?

....

6 Did you have $10 with you? $50? $100?

....

7 Do you like mint flavour chewing gum best? strawberry flavour? lemon flavour?

....

8 Is your flat one kilometre from the centre? two kilometres? three kilometres?

....

B They don't know …

The police are investigating a murder. The detective's notes tell you what they know so far.

What *don't* they know? Write indirect questions beginning *They don't know …*

They don't know what time Sir Hugh came downstairs.
....
....
....
....
....
....
....
....
....
....

Indirect questions	
Where is he?	→ I don't know where he is.
Has he gone out?	→ I'm not sure if/whether he's gone out (or not).
Why did he go?	→ Do you know why he went?

What we know so far

1 Sir Hugh came downstairs <u>some</u> <u>time</u> during the night.
2 He was typing <u>something</u> when he died.
3 <u>Somehow</u> the murderer knew that he would be there.
4 The murderer hit him with <u>something</u>.
5 Sir Hugh <u>either</u> knew the murderer <u>or</u> he didn't.
6 The murderer has hidden the murder weapon <u>somewhere</u>.
7 The murderer is <u>either</u> still in the house <u>or not</u>.
8 <u>Someone</u> killed Sir Hugh.

C Reported questions

These questions were all asked by the same man on the same day – but who did he ask? Complete each sentence using a reported question.

Reported questions

Where is he?	→	She asked me where he was.
Has he gone out?	→	She asked me if/whether he'd gone out.
Why did he go?	→	She asked me why he'd gone.

Can I have the day off on Friday?

Will you pick me up from the office after work?

Have you cleaned your teeth?

When is the world going to end?

When will you be back from lunch?

How long have you been waiting?

Did you have a good day at school?

How much do I have in my account?

1 He asked his 12-year-old daughter *whether she'd had a good day at school.*

2 He asked his wife ....

3 He asked a man at the bus stop ....

4 He asked his secretary ....

5 He asked his bank manager ....

6 He asked his 4-year-old son ....

7 He asked his boss ....

8 He asked a woman with a sandwich board ....

D Question tags

Rewrite these remarks as question tags.

Examples:

I think that's your boss over there. Am I right?
That's your boss over there, isn't it?

In my opinion, that wasn't a very good meal. Do you agree?
That wasn't a very good meal, was it?

Question tags

It's easy, **isn't it?**	You're not going, **are you?**
He'll come, **won't he?**	She won't mind, **will she?**
You saw it, **didn't you?**	You didn't wait, **did you?**
He's gone, **hasn't he?**	I haven't won, **have I?**

1 El Greco wasn't Greek. I don't think so, anyway.

....

2 You haven't met the Prime Minister, as far as I know. Or maybe you have.

....

3 I think he was arrested for shoplifting. Is that right?

....

4 He's a bit strange, in my opinion. What do you think?

....

5 She's always losing her handbag. Have you noticed that?

....

6 Ostriches can't fly. At least I don't think they can.

....

7 I'm sure you won't tell anyone. I hope you won't, anyway.

....

TRANSLATION

Translate into your own language:

1 Do you have any idea what time the train leaves?

....

2 – How long does it take to learn English?
   – That depends on how much you want to learn.

....

....

....

3 – They haven't gone yet, have they?
   – Yes, I think they have, actually.

....

....

Now cover up the left-hand side, and translate your sentences back into English.

LISTENING: Phone conversation

1 ▣ You will hear one side of a phone conversation. Listen and answer the questions.

   – Who is the woman phoning?
   – What are they talking about?
   – What's the problem?

▣ Now rewind and listen again. What do you think the other person says in the gaps?

a ....

....

b ....

....

c ....

....

d ....

....

e ....

....

f ....

....

g ....

....

2 ▣ Now listen to the whole conversation. How close were you?

PRONUNCIATION: Changing tones

1 ▣ Listen to these two-line conversations. Notice the rising and falling tones in the replies. Falling tones are used when we give *new* information; rising tones are used when we *repeat* what has been said before.

a – Did you go abroad this year?

   – I went to New York ↘ in the summer. ↘

b – Did you spend Christmas in New York?

   – No. I went to New York ↗ in the summer. ↘

c – Did you spend the summer in London?

   – No. I went to New York ↘ in the summer. ↗

2 Mark the two parts of the replies with ↘ or ↗ .

a – What's Jim doing at university?

   – He's studying French   at university.

b – What's Jim doing now?

   – He's studying French   at university.

c – Are you still engaged?

   – No. We got married   on Saturday.

d – Did you go out yesterday evening?

   – No. I stayed at home   last night.

e – Do you see much of Ian?

   – Oh, I see him   almost every day.

▣ Now listen and practise saying the conversations.

READING: A bit of luck

She put a bunch of flowers on the station bookstall while she opened her purse, and the flowers started sliding towards the edge. I put out a hand to stop them and she gave me a quick, warm smile. Then she picked up her magazine and flowers, and walked away.

And then, when I got on the train, there she was, with an empty seat beside her.

'Anybody sitting here?' I asked.

She looked up from her magazine. 'No, it's all right,' she said.

So I sat there. I wanted to start a conversation, but I didn't know what to say. It was ridiculous. Then I looked at the luggage rack. Her flowers were there. And her small blue suitcase. I read the initials on the suitcase. The letters were Z.Y. Unusual, I thought.

The train started, and as we left the station she stood up and pushed at the window.

'Here, let me help you,' I said. I jumped up and pushed the window open wide.

'I was trying to close it,' she smiled. So of course I apologised and closed the window. And from then on it was easy. We were speaking to each other.

'Going on holiday?' I asked.

'No,' she said. 'I'm just going to spend a few days with my parents.'

'Me too,' I said. 'For a week.'

When the attendant came, I offered her a coffee. 'Thanks,' she said. 'I haven't had a drink since four.'

We talked for a while, and then she stood up and took her things from the rack. I asked her if she was getting out, and she said yes, she had to change trains.

'I hope I'll see you again,' I said.

And she said yes, she hoped so too. And then she was gone. As the train left the station, I suddenly realised how stupid I had been. I hadn't asked her name. I didn't know where she lived. I didn't know where she worked. I could walk about the city for years and never see her again.

And I just *had* to meet her again. But how? What did I know about her? Well, her initials were Z.Y. What name could I make out of that? Zoe Yeadon? Zenobia Yarrow? I had no idea.

When I got back to the city, I looked through the phone book. There were a few pages of Ys, but not one had a Z in front of it.

It seemed hopeless. I thought back. What else did I know about her? She had a case with her initials on it. She also had a bunch of flowers. Flowers!

She couldn't have bought them that morning, because the shops didn't open till nine, and we had caught the 8.50. But wait a minute – there was a flower stall on the west side of the station, and that was open. And to see the stall, she must have approached the station from the west side.

Which buses stopped on the west side of the station? I checked. There were three routes, all of which went to the suburbs of the city. Well, that narrowed it down to a quarter of a million people.

What else did I remember? The bookstall. She had bought a magazine. What magazine? I didn't know. But I did remember the shelf where she had picked it up. I went back to the bookstall and had a look. The *Builder's Gazette*, *Hi-Fi Illustrated*, the *Teacher's Monthly* ... Could she have been a teacher? No – it was a school day when she travelled. The *Electronics Review*, the *Nursing Journal* ... was she a nurse?

And then it hit me. On the train, she said she hadn't had a coffee since four. Four a.m. She'd just come off night duty.

I looked again at the bus routes. One of them passed a hospital. The Royal Infirmary.

I stood in the hospital drive-way, and wondered where I should try first. I saw a door marked *Enquiries*, and was just walking towards it when an ambulance came racing through the gates. I don't know why I didn't get out of the way in time. I just felt the wing hit me, and then I felt nothing more till I woke up in bed saying, 'Where am I?'

'You're in hospital,' said a nurse.

'Is there a nurse here with the initials Z.Y.?'

'That's me,' she said. 'Zena Yates. Why?'

'You can't be,' I said. 'There can't be two people in any one hospital with the initials Z.Y.'

I lay there for hours. Thinking. And then the simple solution struck me. I asked if I could talk to Zena Yates again.

'Yes,' she said, in answer to my question. 'I lent a little weekend case to one of the other nurses. Her name's Valeria Watson.'

And at last she was there, sitting beside my bed, with just a trace of amusement at the corner of her mouth.

'How did you find me?' she asked.

'Luck,' I said, smiling. 'I had a bit of luck.'

Adapted from the short story *Elementary, My Dearest Watson*, by Eric Bean.

1 *a* Where did the writer first meet the woman?
   b What did he realise after she had got off the train?

2 How did these things help the man to find the woman again?
   – flowers?
   – a bookstall/magazine?
   – a cup of coffee?
   – initials on a suitcase?

3 'Yes,' she said, in answer to my question.
   What do you think the question was?

4 What was the name of the woman in the train?

22 Speaking personally

A Three ways of talking about feelings

1 Complete the table with the missing forms.

2 Now fill the gaps in these sentences with suitable words from the table.

Verb	I feel …	I find it …
annoy	annoyed	annoying
	depressed	
		embarrassing
excite		
	frightened	
relax		
		upsetting
worry		

a I wish they wouldn't have their TV on so loud. It really _annoys_ me.

b I was just walking out when I realised I hadn't paid the bill. It was really ....

c Children are often .... of the dark.

d People often feel .... if they spend too much time just sitting around doing nothing.

e Why don't you just sit down and .... for a few minutes?

f The thought of jumping out of a plane with a parachute .... a lot of people, but I love it – it's so incredibly ....!

g They were very .... when their dog got run over.

h I hate *karaoke*. I get so .... when I have to stand up and sing in front of everybody.

i Don't ....! I'm sure they'll be here soon.

j I love spending the evening in bed reading a good book. I find it very ....

B A time when …

Choose two of the topics in the box and say what happened.

Example:

The other day I bumped into another car at a set of traffic lights. Not much damage was done, but the other driver got really angry. He started shouting at me, and I thought he was going to hit me. Eventually I managed to calm him down: I told him that it was all my fault and that I would pay for the damage.

> A time when …
> … someone tried to persuade you to do something.
> … you tried to cheer someone up.
> … you apologised.
> … you tried to calm someone down.
> … you complained about something.
> … you got angry.

1 ....

....

....

....

....

2 ....

....

....

....

....

C Good and bad

These questions all refer to the words in the box.

1 Write down three words that mean 'very good'.

....
....
....

2 Write down three words that mean 'very bad'.

....
....
....

3 What word(s) best describes:

a a lecture in which you fell asleep?

....

b a TV programme that made you laugh?

....

c a film that kept you on the edge of your seat?

....

d a book that wasn't as good as you thought it would be?

....

awful	entertaining	amusing
boring	fascinating	terrible
brilliant	disappointing	terrific
exciting	dreadful	wonderful

4 Which word could replace the words in italics?

'He told me some *extremely interesting* stories.'

....

New words

Use this space to write down new words from the unit, with your own notes and examples.

....
....
....
....
....
....
....
....
....
....
....
....
....

TRANSLATION

Translate into your own language:

1 He's always complaining about
   everything. I find it really annoying.

....

....

2 Why don't you take him out to see a
   film? That might cheer him up a bit.

....

....

3 It was a very exciting match. Mendes
   played absolutely brilliantly, I thought.

....

....

Now cover up the left-hand side, and translate your sentences back into English.

LISTENING: James Bond films

1 Here are some statements about James Bond
   films. Which do you agree with? Mark your
   own opinion in Column A (✓, ✗ or ?).

		A	B
a	They're enjoyable to watch.		
b	They're really exciting.		
c	Sean Connery is a very good actor.		
d	The early films were the best.		
e	They show women in a negative way.		
f	The stories and characters are unrealistic.		
g	The gadgets and stunts are stupid.		

2 ▭ You will hear three people talking about
   James Bond films. Which opinions does each
   speaker express? Write 1, 2 or 3 in Column B.
   Which speaker do you agree with most?

3 a What does Speaker 1 say that means
      – he's too old for James Bond films?
      – they seem old-fashioned?

   b What does Speaker 2 say that means
      – they have nothing to do with real life?
      – you can forget about everything else?

   c What does Speaker 3 say that means
      – the music in the film was very good?
      – they were very similar to the books?

PHRASAL VERBS: Three-word verbs (2)

1 ▭ Listen to the recording, and complete the three-
   word verbs you hear.

   a put ....   d look ....

   b look ....   e look ....

   c get ....   f stand ....

2 ▭ Now listen again, and try to guess the meaning
   of each verb. Write the meaning in your own
   language. Then use a dictionary to check your
   answers.

3 Fill the gaps with three-word verbs.

   a Everyone .... him
      because he's intelligent.

   b Once I .... writing
      the letter, I found it quite easy.

   c She .... everyone
      who's poorer than herself.

   d My flat .... the
      main square, so it's terribly noisy.

   e It's all we've got to eat, so I'm afraid you'll just
      have to .... it.

   f She was attacked in the press, but all her colleagues
      .... her.

*See also the Phrasal verbs reference section on the last
page of the book.*

WRITING SKILLS: Sequence: unexpected events

1 **Look at these pairs of sentences. Which sentence in each pair is about**
   – a normal sequence of events?
   – something sudden and unexpected?

   1 a Soon *after* the plane *took off*, they started serving drinks.
     b The plane *had just taken off when* smoke started pouring out of the engine.

   2 a *While* I *was getting* ready for bed, I listened to the news on the radio.
     b I *was just getting* ready for bed when I felt a terrible pain in my chest.

   3 a *Before* he *put* his shoes on, he washed his feet carefully in cold water.
     b He *was just about to put* his shoes on *when* he noticed a scorpion inside one of them.

2 **Fill the gaps with suitable expressions, using structures from Part 1.**

   a He .... when
      someone shouted, 'Don't! It's got poison in it!'

   b .... she put
      the receipt in her pocket and went out.

   c I .... when I
      suddenly realised I'd left the front door open.

   d .... when the
      power went off.

   e .... I wiped
      my shoes carefully on the doormat.

3 **Join these sentences to make a story, adding the sentences from the box where you think they fit. Make any changes you think are necessary.**

The telephone rang.

A voice said, 'Meet me downstairs in ten minutes – it's important.'

I put my coat on.

The phone rang again.

The same voice said, 'Walk straight across the street to the other side.'

I heard the sound of a car accelerating.

I ran as fast as I could.

A Mercedes drove past, missing me by inches.

| I'd just come home. |
| I was just going out of the door. |
| I was crossing the street. |
| I'd just reached the pavement. |

....

....

....

....

....

....

....

....

....

....

....

....

23 The unreal past

A What would you have done?

Would you have behaved in the same way as these people?
What would (or wouldn't) you have done?

Example:

After their picnic, Steve and Janet drove home, leaving their rubbish under a tree.

I wouldn't have left my rubbish lying around. I would have taken it home.

1 After waiting half an hour for the waiter to bring his lunch, Mike just carried on reading his paper.

....

....

2 When Claire's six-year-old son fired his water-pistol at her guests and started pulling their hair, she smiled and said 'He loves playing with grown-ups.'

....

....

3 An old lady with two large suitcases was taking a long time to get on the train. George was in a hurry, so he pushed her out of the way and got on the train.

....

....

4 When Helen got bitten on the leg by a poisonous snake, she ran screaming to the nearest village, two kilometres away.

....

....

B Third conditionals

Complete these sentences.

Example: England would have won the match …

… if they hadn't given away that penalty.
… if the referee had been awake.
… if Hodges hadn't been sent off.

> **Third conditionals**
>
> If + Past perfect tense … would(n't) have
> **If I'd known, I wouldn't have gone.**
> The play **would have been** much better if the actors **had learned** their lines.

1 I would have bought that painting ....

2 If I'd known they were vegetarians ....

3 .... we would have been run over.

4 Your bike wouldn't have been stolen ....

5 If you hadn't kicked the dog ....

6 .... I would have smacked him round the face.

7 The party would have been much more fun ....

C It's all your fault

The people in the left-hand pictures wish they were in the right-hand pictures, and each thinks it's the other's fault. Write down what each person is saying, using a mixed conditional.

> **Mixed 2nd and 3rd conditionals**
>
> If you'd gone to college, you'd have a good job now.
> If you hadn't left school at 15, you wouldn't be unemployed.
>
> If we'd left earlier, we wouldn't be stuck in this traffic jam.
> If we hadn't left so late, we'd be on the beach by now.

1 (reserve some seats) *If you'd reserved some seats, we wouldn't be standing in this queue.*

   (get here sooner) ....
   .... *we'd be inside the cinema by now.*

2 (pack some blankets) ....
   ....

   (fill up with petrol) ....
   ....

3 (wear a mask) ....
   ....

   (drop the money) ....
   ....

4 (bring the right equipment) ....
   ....

   (be more careful) ....
   ....

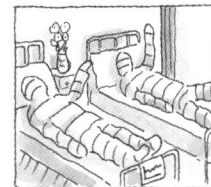

D It's all my own fault

Later on, the people in situations 1–4 above stop arguing, and realise that everything was their own fault.

What regrets do you think they might have? Write three or four sentences for each, using *wish* and *should*. You can use the ideas in Exercise C and/or your own ideas.

> **wish and should**
>
> I wish I'd gone to college.
> I wish I hadn't left school at 15.
>
> We should have left earlier.
> We shouldn't have left so late.

Situation 1

I wish I hadn't arrived so late.

I should have reserved some seats.

I wish I'd gone with someone else.

We should have gone to a restaurant instead.

....

Situation 2

....
....
....
....

Situation 3

....
....
....
....

Situation 4

....
....
....
....

TRANSLATION

Translate into your own language:

1 I certainly wouldn't have invited him
if I'd realised what he was really like.

....

....

2 – How stupid of me. I should have
asked him what his name was.
– I wish you had.

....

....

....

3 You should have been more careful.
Then it would never have happened.

....

....

Now cover up the left-hand side, and translate your sentences back into English.

LISTENING: A better place

1 You will hear five people saying what they
think would make the world a better place.

 Each speaker uses one word from
Column A and one from Column B. Listen and
match the words together. Write a sentence
showing the connection between them.

A	*B*
listen	injuries
water	babies
men	exhaust
cars	other people
guns	oil

2 Listen again. Which of these sentences
gives the best summary of each speaker's
opinion?

1 *a* We often don't notice how others are
feeling.
b People are often less happy than we
realise.

2 *a* Hydro-power is cheaper than oil.
b We could use the world's resources in a
less destructive way.

3 *a* Men don't understand enough about
small children.
b By having babies, men would learn to be
more caring.

4 *a* Exhaust fumes damage the environment.
b Cars make life dangerous and unpleasant.

5 *a* Guns are very destructive.
b We spend too much money on guns.

PRONUNCIATION: Common suffixes

1 Listen to these common endings.

-al	original, professional
-able	comfortable, suitable
-ous	famous, nervous
-ive	passive, attractive
-ent	violent, convenient
-ment	punishment, argument
-or	actor, survivor
-ion	information, television
-ity	university, electricity
-ful	careful, wonderful
-ture	picture, culture

2 How do you think these words are pronounced?

furniture	invention	engagement
helpful	processor	exhibition
previous	precious	individual
confident	sociable	decision
security	positive	qualification
conscious	official	advertisement

 Now listen and practise saying the words.

READING: If things had been different …

Here are one person's regrets. What can you tell about him? Look at the statements below and write *T* (= True), *F* (= False) or *?* (= can't tell).

a	He and his wife have two children.
b	His wife is Spanish.
c	He lives on the island where he grew up.
d	He speaks Spanish well.
e	He can play the drums.
f	He regrets growing up on a small island.
g	He's never lived outside Europe.
h	He learnt Latin at school.
i	He doesn't see his baby during the day.
j	He always does things at the last minute.
k	He's got a piano at home.
l	He's lived in Italy.
m	His wife would like to live abroad.

When I left university, I planned to live in at least five very different countries in at least three different continents. In fact, I only got to live in two, both in Europe, before returning to the UK. Now I'm older, and thoughts of living far away are definitely dreams rather than plans.

I regret the fact that I've always got things done by leaving them until it's nearly too late, and then going mad trying to do it in next to no time. I've learnt to accept that that's the way I am, but I still find I'm always wishing I had done things earlier when there was more time.

I regret giving up the piano about six months after I started learning. My parents told me I would regret it when I was older, but I was about 12, and not bothered by this thought. A few years later, I started playing the drums. I really loved playing them, and became quite good. It would be much easier to have a piano in my house now than a set of drums – they're so impractical and anti-social.

It's a pity that I went to a school where Latin and Greek were not offered as subjects. I've often wanted to know more about the origins of many of the words in English. It would have helped me with other European languages too.

I lived for nearly five years in Spain, but unfortunately I was never in a situation where a Spanish family invited me to their Christmas celebrations, and I've never been to a wedding in Spain. I think Spanish people have a wonderful sense of celebration, and I'm sure these things would have been very enjoyable. Perhaps I should have married a Spanish woman.

I already regret missing so many hours of the first months of my baby's life. He's eight months old now, and I've got used to not seeing him all day, but when he was very small I just wanted to be with him the whole time. I was terrified of missing anything. This feeling began, sadly really, when he was three hours old. My wife had to rest, and there was nothing for me to do but leave them at the hospital and go home.

I wish I'd learnt more German during the ten months I spent in Berlin. I found it too easy to make friends who spoke English. I became reasonably good at shopping, and can still remember words for things like 'horseradish'. But now my German's all gone, and I just get confused when I hear it.

I grew up on a fairly small island. I always regretted not living on the 'mainland'. When I first went to the mainland I felt as if I'd seen very little of life compared to everyone else. I used to be amazed by going on trains, or being able to see more than five kilometres of land in front of me. Now I don't regret it at all – it means I have a beautiful, peaceful place to visit my parents in every year.

24 Life on Earth

A Environment quiz

Write the answers to questions 1–10 in the diagram. Then read the answer to number 11 (going down).

1 The gradual warming up of the Earth is called '............ warming'.

2 Acid .... destroys trees and kills fish in lakes.

3 The hole in the .... layer may cause an increase in skin cancer.

4 Electricity is produced in .... stations.

5 The waste from this kind of *4* station remains dangerous for hundreds of years.

6 Many factories dump dangerous .... straight into the sea.

7 Burning things releases .... dioxide into the atmosphere.

8 The exhaust fumes from cars and lorries cause serious .... in many cities around the world.

9 A good example of the problem of desertification is the .... Desert.

10 Huge areas of tropical rain .... are disappearing every year.

11 Some gases trap the heat from the Sun in the Earth's atmosphere, making the Earth warmer. This is called the '............ effect'.

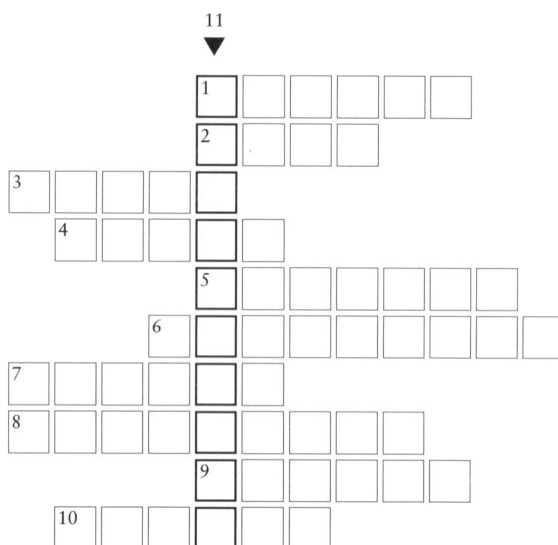

B Agree or disagree?

Do you agree or disagree with these statements? Write a sentence or two saying why, or why not.

Example: Factories should pay a 'pollution tax' – the more they pollute the environment, the more they pay.

I think this is a good idea. It would make pollution expensive, and so factories would try to pollute the environment less. Their products would be more expensive at first, but then the price would come down again.

1 Private cars should be banned from city centres.

....

....

....

2 There will never be another accident with a nuclear power station.

....

....

....

3 The size of newspapers should be limited to 20 pages.

....

....

....

C How green are you?

How green are you in your everyday life? Write about the things you do that are good – and bad – for the environment. Use the illustration to help you. (The self-study listening task on page 110 will help too.)

....

....

....

....

....

....

....

....

....

....

....

New words

Use this space to write down new words from the unit, with your own notes and examples.

....

....

....

....

....

....

....

....

....

....

....

....

....

....

TRANSLATION

Translate into your own language:

1 They've developed a car that runs on solar power.

....
....

2 We need to reduce air pollution by at least ten per cent per year.

....
....

3 The orang-utan is an endangered species, and could become extinct within the next 50 years.

....
....
....

Now cover up the left-hand side, and translate your sentences back into English.

LISTENING: How green are you?

You will hear three people answering the question 'How green do you think you are in your everyday life?'

1 🔲 **Listen and complete the table. (Write ✔, ✗ or ?) Then give each person a score out of 10.**

Do they ...	1	2	3
... try to buy 'green' products?			
... try not to waste paper?			
... try not to waste plastic?			
... avoid travelling by car?			
... recycle glass and paper?			
Score:			

2 🔲 **Listen again and answer the questions.**

a What does Speaker 1 say about
   – CFC gases?
   – shopping bags?

b What does Speaker 2 say about
   – brushing his teeth?
   – wearing a jumper?

c What does Speaker 3 say about
   – paper at school?
   – empty cans?

PHRASAL VERBS: Review

1 **Match these sentences with the continuations in the box.**

a We set off ...
b I'd better get down ...
c I can't work out ...
d I was looking after ...
e Could you pick me up ...
f The café looks out ...
g I could do with ...
h I was in a shop when I ran into ...

... to my homework.
... from the station.
... some new clothes.
... the answer.
... on a large lake.
... on our journey.
... an old friend.
... their baby.

2 **Complete these sentences, using a suitable phrasal verb from the box.**

a I trusted her, but then she ...
b The plane taxied along the runway and ...
c Give me those letters. I'll ...
d If you run you might ...
e I don't need these shoes. I think I'll ...
f She helps me with everything. I couldn't ...
g She's always complaining. Why do you ...
h Her boyfriend's left her. I hope she ...

deal with
catch up with
let down
take off
get over
do without
give away
put up with

🔲 **Now listen and compare what you hear with your own answers.**

See also the Phrasal verbs reference section on the last page of the book.

WRITING SKILLS: Organising ideas

1 Look at these paragraphs.

In most parts of the world, typewriters have been replaced by word processors. Word processors allow you to make changes and corrections as you go along. You can also store a text (a business letter, for example), and use it again at a later date.

In most parts of the world, typewriters have been replaced by word processors. The main advantage of word processors is that they allow you to make changes and corrections as you go along. You can also store a text (a business letter, for example), and use it again at a later date.

Frogs and toads, which used to be common throughout the world, are becoming quite rare species. Ponds and marshes are being turned into farmland, and water throughout the world is becoming more acid as a result of air pollution.

Frogs and toads, which used to be very common, are becoming quite rare species. One reason for this is that ponds and marshes are being turned into farmland. But a more important reason is that water throughout the world is becoming more acid as a result of air pollution.

In what way are the second paragraphs clearer than the first?

2 Look at these opening sentences, and choose suitable continuations for each. Start with one of the expressions from the table, and make any other necessary changes.

a I think the government's plan to build a new city by-pass is very short-sighted. ....
....
....

b It was surprisingly easy for white settlers to occupy land in North America. ....
....
....

c Large dogs aren't very good pets if you live in a small flat. ....
....
....

d I really enjoy speeding along the motorway in my new Porsche. ....
....
....

e I'd much rather be a free-lance journalist than work for a newspaper. ....
....
....

One	reason (for)	
Another	advantage (of)	
The	disadvantage (of)	...
The main	result (of)	
The only	problem (with)	

Continuations:

The Indians had no sense of private property, so they gave land away or sold it very cheaply.

I can work as much or as little as I want to.

Even more people will travel by car instead of cycling or using public transport.

It uses up an enormous amount of petrol.

They need at least an hour's exercise a day.

3 Choose one of the pairs of sentences. Develop it into a paragraph by adding one or two more sentences.

1 Sentence rewriting

Rewrite these sentences using the words given.

Example:
They deliver 300 million letters every day.
300 million letters *are delivered every day.*

1 I bought this typewriter when I left school.

.... since ....

2 They started watching TV four hours ago.

.... four hours.

3 The volcano hasn't erupted for 500 years.

It's 500 years ....

4 Where does she live? I've no idea.

I've no idea ....

5 'Did you lock the front door?' he asked me.

.... whether ....

6 I didn't have enough money, so I didn't buy it.

If ....

7 I should have apologised.

I wish ....

2 Asking questions

Complete the questions.

Example:
– Where *do you work*?
– At Barclays Bank in the High Street. I'm a secretary.

1 – .... learning Chinese?

– For three years. I'm getting pretty fluent now.

2 – .... my glasses, have you?

– Yes I have. They're on the shelf in the bathroom.

3 – What .... like?

– Strawberry, if they've got it. Otherwise, vanilla.

4 – What make ....?

– A Volvo. I've only just bought it.

5 – How .... there by bus?

– About six hours. But it's much quicker by train.

6 – Could you tell me ....?

– The station? Yes, it's just up there on the right.

7 – Penguins live ....?

– No, they don't. The live at the *South* Pole.

3 Vocabulary

1 **What are these words associated with? Mark them**
   B (= birth), M (= marriage) or D (= death).

bridegroom	coffin	midwife
cemetery	funeral	mourning
christen	honeymoon	reception

2 **Match the items on the left with those on the right.**

ambitious	behaves like a child
naughty	gets embarrassed easily
self-conscious	dislikes authority
rebellious	knows a lot about life
wise	wants to be Prime Minister

3 **How do you think these people are feeling?**

a ....   c ....

b ....   d ....

4 **Find pairs of words in the two columns that have**
   similar meanings.

entertaining	dreadful
dull	fascinating
terrible	boring
terrific	amusing
interesting	brilliant

5 **Complete these sentences.**

a .... rain kills trees.

b There's a hole in the ozone ....

c Scientists are worried about the ....

effect, which is causing .... warming.

d As more tropical .... are cut down,

more endangered species become ....

e Chernobyl was a nuclear .... station.

4 Fill the gaps

Fill each gap with *one* suitable word. Example:

I ....*was*............. walking through the park yesterday when I suddenly ....*heard*......... a loud scream.

1 It seems strange to me that at 18 I'm .... to join the army and go and .... for my country, but I'm not old .... to go into a bar and buy a drink. I think the .... should be changed.

2 I .... waiting for my bus last night .... a man drove up and asked me .... long I'd .... waiting. I told him I'd only been there .... a few minutes. He then asked if I .... like a lift. When I ...., he began to .... angry, but just then the bus arrived and he drove ....

3 If that asteroid hadn't .... the Earth 65 million years ago, things might .... turned out very differently. Dinosaurs wouldn't have .... extinct, and maybe the .... race would never have evolved. And the Earth would be a .... cleaner place .... it is today.

5 Writing paragraphs

Write a short paragraph (2 or 3 sentences) on the following:

1 Would you rather be a baby, a child, a teenager, an adult, middle-aged or old? Why?

....
....
....

2 Write about a time when you got angry or upset.

....
....
....

3 Think of a film you saw recently. What was it like? Write a short review.

....
....
....

4 What do you think is the most serious environmental problem? What should be done about it?

....
....
....

6 Dictation

You will hear someone talking about a horror film he saw recently.

Listen and write down what you hear.

Tapescripts

Unit 13 Living in Britain

1 The thing that I find very annoying is separate taps for cold and hot water, because when you haven't got any plug at hand and you want to wash your hands, you simply, you know, either boil your hands using the tap for hot water or you turn your hands into two pieces of ice using the other one. And another thing is left-hand-side driving which makes driving impossible for me because I really can't change gears with my left hand. And I also find it very difficult to cross the street because I always feel very surprised seeing the car coming from the direction which I really don't expect it to come.

2 What is quite different, I think so, is how polite English people are compared to French people. Just, for example, when you're in the street and then you just suddenly bump into someone and the way people say 'Oh I'm really sorry, excuse me, dear'. Or even when you're queueing somewhere, the English people just go in the queue and just wait for, they just wait quietly and don't say anything.

3 I think that the strangest thing that I've noticed, especially lately, is that people have an attitude here to possibly the way you speak and definitely the way that you dress. For example, I was in town the other day, it was a very, very sunny day and I'd just finished work and I went for a swim and when I was walking home I was walking in my cut-off shorts and I had no shoes and socks and a towel and a T-shirt and the amount of people that stared at me as if they'd never seen a pair of shorts before or somebody with no shoes and socks before, struck me as strange.

Unit 14 Media habits

1 A What newspaper do you read mostly?
   B I read *The Scotsman*, which is, I think, Scotland's biggest national newspaper. I like it because it's very interesting for local news, but at the same time it has very good coverage of other British news items, and it's good for international news as well.
   A Do you read any weekly magazines?
   B Um yes, I read *The Economist*, which is closely associated with my work.
   A What about television? What do you watch on television?
   B Well unfortunately I don't watch very much television. I find I don't really have enough time for that.

And in fact I spend a lot more time listening to the radio, I think really because I find I can do other things at the same time as listening to the radio. On the radio I always listen to the news, probably two or even three times a day, and news discussion programmes.

2 A What newspapers do you read?
   B Well I buy *The Times* because it's got a really good crossword, and I can't get through the day without the *Times* crossword.
   A Do you read any weekly magazines?
   B Yes I get the magazine called the *New Scientist,* which is essentially about news in science around the world, and that's just because I'm interested in science generally.
   A What about television? What do you watch on television?
   B I like watching movies, especially if they're thrillers or detective movies, that kind of thing, where I can just sit down for the evening and relax.
   A Do you listen to the radio at all?
   B Yeah, all the time, even when I'm working. Again I prefer talking radio rather than just music, music, music. And I find that I can work and listen to the radio at the same time.

Unit 14 Phrasal verbs

1 He gave all his money away.
2 He gave away the plans to the enemy.
3 The music's too loud – could you turn it down?
4 They offered him the job, but he turned it down.
5 His parents brought him up much too strictly.
6 I decided to bring up the question of pay at the meeting.
7 I looked up Botswana in the atlas.
8 You must look me up if you're ever in London.
9 Pick up that bag – you dropped it.
10 I'll pick you up at 5.30 and we'll go there together.
11 They've put up a huge block of flats near the station.
12 You don't need to stay in a hotel – we can put you up for the night.

Unit 15 What has happened?

1 A Karl, it was a really good party last night. (Thanks) Terrific. But look, I've lost one of my earrings.
   B Oh no, you're joking. Where?
   A Well, I'm not sure, it could be anywhere. (Um) It looks like a blue dolphin.
   B Right, well, do you know which room you spent most time in last night?

   A No, anywhere really.
   B Well, did you dance?
   A Yes, (Right) a lot.
   B OK, well you probably lost it there. I tell you what, I'll have a look in the lounge, and then I'll ring you back, yeah?
   A Oh thanks a lot.
   B All right.

2 A Hi Sue, it's me.
   B How did you get on?
   A I've passed.
   B Oh Chris, that's brilliant news.
   A Oh God, yeah, I'm so pleased, it's such a relief.
   B Third time lucky, eh?
   A Third time lucky. I wasn't sure I was going to do it at all, but ah, I'm so relieved …
   B What was the examiner like?
   A He was really nice actually. He made me feel really relaxed early on. And I didn't really have any problems.
   B What about your parking and your reversing?
   A No that was all fine. I was just so much more relaxed this time.
   B Oh, you must feel over the moon.
   A Yeah, as a celebration, I'm going to take you out for a drive over the weekend. What do you reckon? (Oh superb)

3 A Listen, I've got a real problem.
   B What is it?
   A The car's broken down.
   B Oh not again.
   A Yeah, I checked the oil, and I checked the battery. It's not, I don't know what it is, it's just not starting at all.
   B You'll have to get rid of it you know.
   A I know, I know. But look, the thing is, I've got to pick Samantha up at the airport.
   B Do want to borrow mine?
   A Do you mind? (No) I know I'm covered by the insurance.
   B Well you drove it last week, didn't you?
   A Well, that would be a great favour.
   B Oh, come round when you like. I don't need it till tonight.
   A OK, I'll be round in about an hour. (OK) Thanks a lot.

Unit 16 Three school subjects

1 I think my most tedious memory at school was at biology when we had to learn the Latin names of lots of plants and animals, and we'd spend hours looking at them written down on the blackboard and just having to copy them out and remember them. Seemed a real waste of time to me.

2 History was great fun. We didn't have to learn dates – well we had to learn some of course, yes, but we didn't get good or bad marks for knowing or not knowing history. We learned a lot about individuals, famous people, not so famous people, it seemed to all make sense and it felt as if history had a meaning for us. No, it was great, it was good, I enjoyed it and the teachers seemed to make it very realistic and true to life.

3 Well, one of the subjects that I learned at school was history, which I felt very critical about the way that I learned it, because we learned a lot about kings and queens and battles and emperors and things. We never actually really learned that much about people and their everyday lives, and how they survived, how they made a living, how they survived through these wars.

4 Science was not very well taught. It wasn't the fault of the teachers, rather that they didn't have the money to supply the equipment that you need. We just didn't have that. What the teacher would have to do was stand at the front of the class and perform the experiment himself, and we'd just have to watch, we wouldn't have the chance to actually do the experiment ourselves, which would have helped us learn.

Unit 17 Locked in!

Part 1

I went down to Madrid to work for a month for a big company down there, and it was my first Friday, I'd only been there a few days, and they'd cleared out an old storeroom and put a desk in it for me and I was working away and it must have been about five o'clock in the evening when I walked out of my little office, and I realised that everybody had gone home. And the main lights were all out, so I ran downstairs in case I could catch somebody leaving but it was too late, the doors were all locked, and I was stuck. So I ran upstairs again and picked up the phone, one of the phones, and it was dead, so I tried another phone and that phone was dead as well, and clearly they'd switched the phones off for the weekend. So I went to the window and the windows wouldn't open, they were barred, and it was beginning to get dark, and I thought 'Well, I'm here for the weekend.' Anyway, what I did eventually was I went downstairs again to the reception area and the reception was a small room with glass walls and of course it was locked but I noticed that inside there was a phone which had a little red light on it.

Part 2

And there was a cabinet up on the wall in the hallway which was locked of course but it was full of keys. And somehow I managed to break this open and inside there were hundreds of keys,

and I thought 'Well one of them must be the key to this reception area', and I had a box of matches with me fortunately because it was getting really dark now, this was January, and I tried key after key after key and eventually I found a key which fitted this reception area. And I went inside, and there was a list on the wall of a number of phone numbers including the duty officer. And this phone was in fact live, and I picked it up and called this man, and he was pretty cross because he was just going off to the opera I think, but he came round in his dinner jacket and let me out, and so I got home.

Unit 18 A case of fraud

Part 1

I know of an amazing case where a man was charged with fraud. What he'd been doing was, he'd got some headed paper from the British Government and had written to countries like Australia and Canada and South Africa where he knew that a lot of people from England had emigrated and he said in this letter 'We the British Government, if you send us $10, or £10, will trace your lineage and find out your family tree and if we find that anybody in your family going back over the generations was famous or of interest, we will let you know and send you your family tree. A lot of people received this letter and obviously thought 'Well that's interesting' and they sent him $10. And a few months later he would send them a letter back saying 'There's nothing of interest in your family tree.' And they did nothing about it.

Part 2

But he got away with this for a long time but eventually he became greedy and sent so many letters out that it became impossible to answer all the letters, and people started to complain about it and as more and more complaints occurred in each country they started to investigate and discovered this man who had made a fortune out of it. And I think it was rather a shame that he was caught because I think for $10 it's a story worth being involved in really and I think, you know, he only ever took $10 at a time from each person, and I think he deserved to keep it.

Unit 18 Phrasal verbs

a I couldn't possibly do without my computer – I use it all the time.
b I'm dying of thirst – I could really do with a long, cold drink.
c The book deals mainly with the Second World War, but there are some chapters on life in the 1930s.
d She's taking a long time to get over her mother's death – they were very close to each other.
e They're finding it quite hard to cope with bringing up five children – they're thinking of getting a childminder.

f Since my illness, I've really gone off greasy food – even the smell of it makes me feel sick.

Unit 19 Favourite things

1 One of my favourite things is a photograph of my sister and me. It was taken about ten years ago when we were both very young, standing on the beach in our shorts and T-shirt, and it was a very sunny day and we both look very happy in the photograph. And I like to keep this photograph because it's a nice memory and I can look back and remember the fun we used to have when we were younger. So it's something I'd like to keep always.

2 One of my favourite possessions is my camera. I often go out and take photographs. I bought it when I was much younger, about 12 years old, in New York in a second-hand shop. I can remember saving up my money for at least a year beforehand and choosing it very carefully in the window. I use it quite often to go out and take photographs. It's not one of the most expensive cameras that you can buy, and it might now seem quite outdated, but very often what's more important for making nice pictures is your own eye and judgment of the situation rather than how much it costs.

3 One of my favourite things is my wind-up gramophone, you know one of the ones with the big horn. I got that about, oh, seven or eight years ago in Malaysia. I'd been looking for one for a long time in this country, but they're terribly expensive. But I was working in Malaysia, and I found one there in a sort of antique shop, and it was just affordable, so I bought it there. And not only is it a very, I think, beautiful object in its own right, but it also brings back very strong memories of Malaysia for me. And I listen to it quite regularly and I often go out looking for old gramophone records to play on it.

Unit 20 Birth and marriage

Story A

When I was pregnant with my first baby, I read an article in a magazine about having a baby in water. And it was the Russians I think who first decided that this was a good idea, because it said in the paper you didn't feel any pain. So I actually decided that this is what I'd like to do. So I went and looked, tried to find somewhere because, you know, you can't go to your local swimming pool or anything, so I found this company and they hire out these fantastic little swimming pools. And then the difficulty was to find a doctor or a midwife or someone like that who would actually let me give birth to my baby under water. And I found this really, really lovely midwife and I've stayed friends with her ever since. And on the 11th May 1985 my little girl was born, and we never even went near a hospital – it was wonderful.

Story B
A couple of years ago I went to an extraordinary wedding. These two friends of mine tried to think of something different, and what they did was they decided to get married in a circus, so they got married in this circus tent, and invited all their friends to come as – they didn't want anyone to be dressed formally so they, we all went in fancy dress, as gangsters, as whatever, some people went as clowns, obviously, it being a circus. But what was even more extraordinary was when we got to the circus, for the reception, there was the church service and then we went off to the reception in the circus tent, what none of us knew was that the bride and groom had rehearsed for a whole week this trapeze act, and they were going to do it in front of all of us at the beginning of the wedding. So they came on, and did this incredible trapeze act, which I think was one of the most extraordinary weddings I've ever been to.

Unit 21   Phone conversation

A Hello? Hello, is that Mr King? This is Julie Richards.

B Ah yes, you're phoning about the printer, aren't you?

A Yes that's right. Have you had a look at it yet?

B Yes, we have. I'm afraid the motor's burnt out.

A Oh dear. Will you be able to repair it, do you think?

B Oh no, we couldn't repair it. We'd have to put in a new motor.

A I see. And how much would that cost?

B That would be let me see, £245 including labour.

A Oh, that sounds an awful lot. How much would it cost to buy a new printer?

B A new printer would be £320.

A Oh really? It's hardly worth repairing then, is it?

B Well, it isn't really. You might as well get a new one, yeah.

A OK, I think I'll probably have to do that, then.

B Right. Would you like to order one now from us?

A Um, well I'm not sure. I'll think about it. OK, thanks anyway. Bye.

Unit 22   James Bond films

1 I used to find them quite exciting and amusing, but I think I've grown out of them now. They seem a little bit outdated. For example the gadgets they use in them – they were supposed to be the latest inventions and now they seem ridiculous to our generation. And for example you · realise that the stunts they use in the films are very artificial and also the situations in which they put the characters, they're quite forced. But apart from those negative points I think they could be quite enjoyable for some people.

2 I really enjoy James Bond films because they're very exciting and I like all the gadgets that they have and because they're pure escapism, you can really just switch off and enjoy watching them and enjoy the adventure of it. And although I suppose they're very sexist as well, somehow it seems to be OK because they're James Bond films, and it doesn't matter too much.

3 I love them, especially the early ones. *From Russia with Love*, a brilliant film, brilliant theme music, and Sean Connery was a terrific actor in his role as James Bond. And the beauty of the early films was that they followed the books pretty closely. And I had read all of the James Bond novels and so it was very interesting to go and compare of course. And I loved the earlier James Bond, but the later ones not so much. They became more like comedies. I think a lot of people found them entertaining because of that but I didn't like the later ones as much as I liked the earlier ones.

Unit 22   Phrasal verbs

a He always comes home after midnight. I don't know why she puts up with it.

b It's a nice quiet room. It looks out on a small garden.

c Well, it's time to get down to some work. It's nearly 10 o'clock.

d He was a great leader and the whole country looked up to him.

e Just because he hasn't got a job is no reason to look down on him.

f You ought to stand up for yourself. Don't let them tell you what to do.

Unit 23   A better place

1 I think the world would be a better place if everyone listened to each other a bit more. I think we go through life not listening, not taking any notice of how other people are feeling, and how things are upsetting them or if they're happy.

2 I think the world would be a better place if there were, there was no oil to be used for power. The world is seven tenths water. Therefore, those seven tenths water could quite easily make hydro-power. It would be cheaper, it would be cleaner, it would be using the world's resources and raw materials in a positive way, not just burning them and getting rid of them and creating more poison.

3 I think the world would be a better place if men had babies for a change, and they suddenly had to have a whole new kind of experience. It would be very interesting to see how the world might change and improve if they were responsible for the care of babies and families.

4 I think the world would be a much better place if we didn't have so many cars on the road, and also if the speed limit was dropped as well. But it's also the exhaust, the fumes, it's just getting overcrowded, it's just not pleasant to go out for a walk any more.

5 Well I think the world would be a better place if there weren't any guns. Just look at how much they cost and look at the cost in human lives and in injuries and so on caused only because of guns. Yes, no guns.

Unit 24   How green are you?

1 (So how green do you think you are in your everyday life?) I think I do the basic, you know, necessities, I think for example when I go shopping I don't buy products if they've got CFC gases, and I always make sure that they haven't been tested on animals. I think I probably could do a lot more, for example I tend to use paper, I'm not conscious of how much paper I'm using and I know I probably waste a lot. I do drive a car, but that has unleaded petrol in it. Another thing is plastic I think, I'm not conscious of how much plastic I, you know, for example in the supermarkets I don't take my own shopping bags, I tend to use more and more bags each week, and I think that's bad. So I think basically I do as much as I can for myself but if I really made an effort I could do more.

2 (How green do you think you are in your everyday life?) In my everyday life I think I am green. I don't run the tap while I'm brushing my teeth. I will sort out rubbish and take bottles to the bottle bank, paper to the paper bank, etc. But I'm very hypocritical in that I do a lot of driving, and often it's unnecessary driving, in that I'm polluting the atmosphere with the fumes from my vehicle. I'm green from the point of view that I use two sides of a piece of paper. I don't waste paper – I use both sides if I have to. However I do turn the heating up and waste electricity as opposed to putting an extra jumper on.

3 (How green do you think you are in your everyday life?) Well we certainly use green products, I suppose you'd have to call them, around the house, you know, recycled loo paper, recycled kitchen roll, recycled plastic bottles, and we certainly make an effort to recycle anything that we can, like glass jars or glass bottles. In school we have a recycling paper system which I do try and stick to. There's a tray in every classroom, and instead of throwing away paper into a wastepaper-basket you just put the paper in there and it's recycled and collected every week. I'm not as green

as I could be, I think, in the way that I'm quite lazy – if I have a can, you know, which is empty I will throw it in a bin, I won't take it home with me and save it up, you know. But we don't have a car, which is I think a big thing – we all cycle, which is really good. Always take our own shopping bags when we go shopping, which I think we did even before the big green thing came along, you know, for convenience as much as anything else.

Unit 24 Phrasal verbs

a I trusted her, but then she let me down.
b The plane taxied along the runway and took off.
c Give me those letters. I'll deal with them.
d If you run you might catch up with them.
e I don't need these shoes. I think I'll give them away.
f She helps me with everything – I couldn't do without her.
g She's always complaining. Why do you put up with her?
h Her boyfriend's left her. I hope she gets over it soon.

Answer key

Unit 13 Comparing and evaluating

A Small and big differences

1 Cars aren't nearly as dangerous as motorbikes.
2 CDs are slightly more expensive than cassettes.
3 English is much more useful than Greek.
4 French mustard isn't quite as hot as German mustard.
5 The train doesn't take quite as long as the bus.
6 His qualifications aren't nearly as good as mine.

B Comparison of adjectives and adverbs

Adj	good	*AA*	fast
Adv	well	*Adv*	clearly
Adj	friendly	*Adj*	comfortable
AA	hard	*Adj*	funny

1 better
2 better
3 more friendly / friendlier
4 harder
5 faster
6 better/more clearly
7 more comfortable
8 funnier/better

C Too and enough

1 He was too heavy.
  The chair wasn't strong enough.
2 It was too difficult (for him).
  His Spanish wasn't good enough.
3 It was too high (for him to climb).
  He wasn't fit enough.
4 There were too many questions.
  He didn't have enough time.

Listening: Living in Britain

1 separate taps – wash your hands
  cross the street – seeing the car coming
  bump into someone – 'Oh, I'm really sorry'
  left-hand-side driving – change gears
  walking in my shorts – people stared
2 *Speaker 1*
  a The water is either too hot or too cold when she
    washes her hands.
  b Because the gear stick is on the left.
  c Surprised.
  Speaker 2
  a Polite.
  b They wait quietly.
  Speaker 3
  a Cut-off shorts and a T-shirt.
  b Shoes and socks.
  c They thought he looked unusual.

Pronunciation: Linking words: consonant + consonant

2 *a* Is it good luck to see a black cat?
  b The next train to Prague goes in ten minutes.
  c The clock said ten past two.
  d I bought two bedside tables and some red curtains.
  e We had fish soup and French bread.
  f Like most people, I sometimes feel lonely.

Reading: Left-handedness

1 *a* True
  b False
  c True (in the US)
  d True
  e False
  f False
  g False
  h True
2 The tusk it uses more is larger.
3 People don't have as much practice playing against
  left-handed players.
4 *b* and *f*.

Unit 14 The media

A Which page?

2 24	6 21–24	10 6–10	14 18
3 14	7 24	11 17	
4 2–5	8 11–12	12 15–16	
5 18	9 19–20	13 13	

C Understanding the headlines

1 The Mona Lisa has been stolen.
2 A new Shakespeare play has been discovered.
3 A bank manager has disappeared with £1 million.
4 A 12-year-old has climbed Mount Everest.
5 Electricity prices are going to rise by 150%.
6 The White House has been damaged by a bomb.
7 Britain will become a Republic on January 1.
8 A chimpanzee has won a game of chess.

Listening: Media habits

1 *Speaker 1*
  Newspaper: *The Scotsman*
  Magazines: *The Economist*
  TV: not much
  Radio: news, news discussion programmes
  Speaker 2
  Newspaper: *The Times*
  Magazines: *New Scientist*
  TV: movies, especially thrillers
  Radio: news, talk (not music)
2 *a* Both *c* 2 *e* 2 *g* 1
  b 1 *d* Both *f* 2

Phrasal verbs: Double meanings

1 give away	*b, e*	look up	*i, k*
turn down	*h, l*	pick up	*d, g*
bring up	*c, f*	put up	*a, j*

2 1 e   4 l   7 k   10 g
  2 b   5 f   8 i   11 j
  3 h   6 c   9 d   12 a
3 *a* ... turned him down.
  b ... look it up?
  c ... give them away.
  d ... put you up.

e ... turn it down?
f ... look him up?
g ... pick them up.
h ... brought me up.

Writing skills: Similarities

2 *Possible answers:*
  a Tobacco isn't very good for you, and nor is alcohol.
  b Both lions and wolves are dangerous animals.
  c Tokyo, Hong Kong and Singapore are all in the Far East.
  d Abraham Lincoln and John F Kennedy were both assassinated.
4 *Possible answers:*
  a John and Richard are both talented musicians. Both of them have good singing voices, and play several different instruments.
  b Neither Mars nor Jupiter is able to support life. Both planets are very cold, and neither of them has any oxygen in its atmosphere.
  c Christianity, Islam and Buddhism are all major world religions which have spread through many countries. All three have millions of followers, and they have all had a major influence on art and literature.

Unit 15 Recent events

A Personal news

Possible answers:
1 We've finally arrived in Turkey. We got here yesterday morning. It wasn't a very good trip – we broke down twice! Anyway, we've found a lovely little apartment by the sea. The food's good, the sea's really warm, and everyone's very friendly.
2 I've given up smoking! I stopped two weeks ago. It was very difficult at first, but now it's getting much easier. Unfortunately, I'm putting on a lot of weight, but that's not important. The important thing is that I'm never going to smoke again.

B Asking questions

1 How did they get in?
  Have they been caught (yet)?
2 What caused the crash?
  Where did it happen?
  Were the people on board killed?
3 When did they arrive?
  How long did it take to get there?
  Have they sent back any photos?

C What have they been doing?

1 She's been writing letters.
2 They've been doing the housework / cleaning the flat.
3 He's been doing his homework.
4 They've been decorating their flat.
5 She's been getting ready to go out.
6 He's been playing chess.
7 She's been reading the paper.

Listening: What has happened?

1 *a* a party
  b a driving test
  c a car breaking down
2 *1* – The woman's lost an earring.
    – Dancing.
    – He's going to look for it and ring her back.
  2 – Pleased/relieved. He's passed his driving test.
    – It's his third attempt to pass the test.
    – Go for a drive over the weekend.
  3 – The woman's car's broken down.
    – Borrow her friend's car. To pick someone up at the airport.
    – No. The friend says 'Oh not again' and 'You drove it last week, didn't you?'

Pronunciation: Changing stress

2 *a* – I've <u>bought</u> some <u>chocolates</u>.
  b – I've <u>bought</u> some chocolates.
  c – I've <u>been</u> on <u>holiday</u>.
  d – I've been on <u>holiday</u>.
  e – Do you <u>want</u> some <u>orange juice</u>?
  f – Do you want some <u>orange juice</u>?

Reading: Personal letters

1 Alan – writer
  Katrina – teacher
  Jim – musician (horn player)
2 *a* Alan   *d* Jim
  b Katrina   *e* Jim
  c Katrina, Alan *f* Katrina
3 *a* False   *f* True
  b False   *g* Can't tell
  c True   *h* False
  d False   *i* True
  e True

Unit 16 Teaching and learning

A School subjects

1 history   6 geography
2 music   7 biology
3 mathematics   8 languages
4 literature   9 chemistry
5 art   10 timetable

Listening: Three school subjects

1 *B* Latin names   *H* dates
  H famous people   *H* battles
  S equipment   *B* plants
  S experiment   *H* emperors
2 Speaker 1: *c*   Speaker 3: *b*
  Speaker 2: *d*   Speaker 4: *f*

Phrasal verbs: Prepositional verbs (1)

2 look after – care for
look into – investigate
call for – collect, pick up
run into – meet (by chance)
come across – find (by chance)
take after – resemble
take to – like, be attracted to

3 *a* take to   *e* take after
  b came across   *f* call for
  c look after   *g* ran into
  d looking into

Writing skills: Letter writing

1 *a* 5; *b* 2; *c* 4; *d* 3; *e* 1
2 *a* 1; *b* 5; *c* 3; *d* 4; *e* 2
3 A: 4; B: 1, 3; C: 2, 5
4 *Possible answers:*
  1 Dear Sir/Madam,
    I saw your advertisement for Banana T-shirts in the *Evening News*. Please send me two T-shirts, one medium and one large. I enclose a cheque for £30.
    Yours faithfully,
  2 Dear Sir/Madam,
    I'm writing to ask for more information about your luxury campsites in Northern Spain. Please send me a brochure and details of prices and facilities available at the campsites. I look forward to hearing from you.
    Yours faithfully,
  3 Dear Mr Paterson,
    I saw your advertisement in *Boats and Boating* this month, and I'm very interested in working on a yacht this summer. Please send me more information about the jobs you are offering, including details of pay and working conditions. I look forward to hearing from you soon.
    Yours sincerely,

Unit 17 Narration

A What had happened?

Possible answers:
1 The train had left.
2 He had been shot.
3 Someone had locked it.
4 I had been arrested.
5 Someone had taken it.
6 He had had dinner there only the night before.
7 I had taken the bullets out.

B Past states and previous actions

Possible answers:
3 She had bruised her leg.
4 His hands were clean/washed.
5 Someone had switched on the light. / The light had been switched on.
6 The room was tidy.
7 The rain had stopped. / It had stopped raining.
8 They were asleep.

C Reported speech

2 … he/she wouldn't put up taxes.
3 … she had missed the last bus.
4 … they were doing all they could to solve the case.
5 … she didn't want to see him any more.
6 … I was going to have a fantastic week.
7 … he hadn't finished it yet.
8 … I would have to have an operation.

D I realised …

Possible answers:
1 It was two in the morning when Joe was woken up by a crash in the living room. He picked up the statue of Winston Churchill which he kept on his bedside table, and crept along the hall. Then he heard a 'miaow', and realised that it wasn't a burglar – it was the cat, which had knocked over a vase in the dark.
2 At last they were on the road. They'd packed all the suitcases, locked up their flat, and were on their way to the coast. In two hours, thought Helen, they would be on the ferry to France. She felt in her pocket – it was empty. And then she realised that she had left the tickets in the drawer in the hall. She sighed, and turned the car round.

Listening: Locked in!

1 *a* He was working alone in a room.
  b It was locked.
  c They'd switched the phones off for the weekend.
  d They wouldn't open.
  e There was a phone in there with a red light on.
2 cabinet; keys; matches; key; reception area; phone numbers; duty officer; phoned; let him out

Pronunciation: Linking words with /w/ or /j/

2 How interesting   /w/
  So am I   /w/
  My uncle   /j/
  Two or more   /w/
  Any others?   /j/
  High up in the sky   /j/
  No overtaking   /w/
  Blue eyes   /w/

3 *a* They all /j/ went to Amsterdam. /w/
  b Who are /w/ you talking to on /w/ the phone?
  c Go up /w/ that way and /j/ you'll see it. /j/
  d He isn't /j/ very easy /j/ to talk to.
  e How many are /j/ there? Three or /j/ four?

Reading: Strange – but true?

1 *Suggested answers:*
  a Italy, USA
  b Australia, Bangladesh
  c Indonesia
  d Spain, Great Britain
  e Poland, USA

Unit 18 Breaking the law

A Criminals and their crimes

2	burglar	6	murderer
3	hijacker	7	shoplifter
4	smuggler	8	vandal
5	blackmailer	9	kidnapper

Possible crimes:

2 She broke into a house and stole a TV set and a video recorder.
3 He hijacked a plane on its way from London to New York and made the pilot fly to Beirut.
4 He smuggled 100 grams of heroin through customs hidden in a tube of toothpaste.
5 She discovered that a colleague at work had been to prison, and told him she wanted £2,000 to keep quiet about it.
6 Her husband wouldn't give her a divorce, so she pushed him off a cliff.
7 He stole a camera from a department store.
8 She smashed windows in the local school and sprayed paint on the walls.
9 He kidnapped the baby son of a millionaire and demanded a ransom of $500,000.

B Crime story

arrested … charged … trial … prosecution … witnesses … defence … evidence … jury … verdict … guilty … judge … fine … prison … court … innocent

Listening: A case of fraud

2 *a* $10; family tree; family; famous / of interest; family tree
  b nothing of interest; family tree
3 After a time, he became *greedy*, and stopped *answering* letters. People in *each country* started to complain. They investigated, and *discovered* the man. The speaker thinks it's a pity he *was caught*.

Phrasal verbs: Prepositional verbs (2)

2 *a* 3; *b* 6; *c* 5; *d* 2; *e* 4; *f* 1
2 *a* went off   *d* getting over
  b cope with   *e* could do with
  c dealt with   *f* couldn't do without

Writing skills: Defining and non-defining relative clauses

2 *a D*
  b ND   This is my friend Sarah, who I've known …
  c D
  d D
  e ND   Sydney, where I lived for ten years, is …
  f D
3 *Possible answer:*
I was sitting in a café *where* I often go for a drink after work. I called the waiter, *who* I know quite well, *and* asked for a coffee and a ham sandwich. While I was waiting, I looked at a newspaper *which* was lying on the table, *and* started reading an article on the front page. It said, 'Police are looking for a medical student, Veronica Hall, *who* has been missing from her home for two weeks.' I looked at the photograph, *which* showed a young woman with dark, curly hair. It was a face I recognised at once. She was my new next-door neighbour, *who* had moved in just two weeks before.

Review Units 13–18

1 Sentence rewriting

1 I'm not quite as old as my brother. (I'm slightly younger than my brother.)
2 I can run much/far faster than you. (I'm a much faster runner than you.)
3 My son isn't tall enough to reach the light switch.
4 An escaped prisoner has been recaptured by the police.
5 He's not very good at typing.
6 She realised that they had already gone.
7 Someone had broken the window.

2 Verb forms

1 has been destroyed; started; spread; are still searching
2 I've been trying; I've given; have been doing (am doing); I've lost
3 had had; hadn't eaten; started

3 Vocabulary

1 comedy show – makes you laugh
  chat show – stars talking about themselves
  documentary – gives you information
  game show – trying to win prizes
  soap – never-ending drama
2 *a* history
  b geography
  c literature
  d mathematics (science, physics)
  e science
3 primary; secondary; degree; graduate
4 burglary; murderer; blackmail; vandal; robbery
5 the accused – the person on trial
  the defence – want a 'not guilty' verdict
  the judge – the person in charge
  the jury – decide on the verdict
  the prosecution – want a 'guilty' verdict
  the witnesses – give evidence

4 Fill the gaps

1 (news)paper; turn; told; would; had; be
2 wanted; having/taking; how; at; better
3 have; enough; much; to; cooked/made; been

6 Dictation

Yesterday morning, a woman walked into a charity shop carrying a large plastic sack. She told the assistant that it contained clothes that her family no longer needed. She handed over the sack and left.

Later on, she came back, and said that she had given them a coat belonging to her husband by mistake. The assistant explained that all the clothes that had been received that day had already been taken to the charity's head office for checking and cleaning, before being put on sale. The woman seemed very upset, and left immediately.

Meanwhile, an employee at head office was sorting through the sack of clothes when she discovered a number of rings, necklaces and other pieces of jewellery in the pocket of a man's coat. She called the police, and it turned out that the jewellery had been stolen from a local jeweller's shop in a robbery only the night before, and was worth nearly £300,000.

Police are now searching for the woman – and her husband – and expect to arrest them very soon.

Unit 19 Up to now

A Duration

1 *a* known; for   *b* been learning; for
  c had; since   *d* been playing; since
2 *a* Gary and Eileen have been engaged since July 1985.
  b Henry Palmer has been having driving lessons (has been learning to drive) for 20 years / since his 17th birthday.
  c Tom Kemp has been chewing (has had) the same piece of chewing gum for two years.
  d Ken Garret has been living in the garage since last October.
3 *a* They've been engaged since Eileen left school.
  b He's been having driving lessons since he was 17.
  c He's been chewing the same piece of chewing gum since he scored the winning goal in the Cup Final.
  d He's been living in the garage since he had an argument with his wife.

B How long (ago) …?

1 How long have you been living in Beverly Hills?
  How long ago did you make your first film?
2 How long ago did you join the company?
  How long have you been President?
Possible answers:
3 How long have you been playing with the band?
  How long ago did you learn to play the guitar?

Listening: Favourite things

1 a; photograph; beach; shorts and T-shirt
  b; camera; 12 years old; second-hand; outdated
  d; gramophone; wind-up; big horn
2 1 About ten years ago.
    The speaker and her sister.
    It's a nice memory.
  2 When he was 12 years old, in New York.
    He saved up for a year.
  3 Seven or eight years ago in Malaysia.
    It's beautiful, and it reminds him of Malaysia.

Pronunciation: Stress and suffixes

2 *a* politics   political
  b electric   electricity
  c mystery   mysterious

d examined   examination
e alcohol   alcoholic

Reading: Four logic puzzles

1 Quentin's; She's hurt her eye.
  (From left to right, the patients are: Richard, Quentin, Ursula, Tom, Sue.)
2 Three years; he's 33.
3 Alice and Cecil live on Alithia; they've been married for nine years, and have three children.
  Brian and Delia live on Pseudia; they've been married for ten years and have one child.

4

Jim	*Kate*	*Laura*	*Mike*
teacher	electrician	doctor	baker
2 years	1 year	4 years	3 years
1 week ago	1 week ago	2 weeks ago	2 weeks ago
Kate	Jim	Mike	Laura
lost	won	won	lost

Unit 20 In your lifetime

A | F | r | o | m | c | r | a | d | l | e | t | o | g | r | a | v | e |

midwife; birth; born; mother
  christened
brides; married; wedding; religious; office
  reception; honeymoon
age; buried; cremated; heaven; funeral

C What are they like?

1 naughty   4 lonely   7 shy
2 ambitious   5 self-conscious   8 helpless
3 wise   6 independent   9 rebellious

Listening: Birth and marriage

1 *B* trapeze act   *A* Russians
  A pregnant   *A* swimming pool
  B groom   *B* circus tent
  A midwife   *B* bride
  B clowns   *A* hospital
  A pain   *B* reception
2 *a* … in water.
  b … you don't feel any pain.
  c … little swimming pool.
  d … midwife.
  e … had a baby girl.
  f … get married in a circus.
  g … in fancy dress.
  h … did a trapeze act.
  i … rehearsing/practising.

Phrasal verbs: Three-word verbs (1)

2 *a* … on cigarettes.
  b … with my work.
  c … for cars.
  d … with the others.
  e … of sugar.

3 *a* catch up with   *d* get on with
  b cut down on   *e* run out of
  c look out for

Writing skills: Joining ideas: showing what's coming next

1 *a5*; *b3*; *c2*
2 *a* Fortunately
  b Not surprisingly
  c Surprisingly
  d On the other hand
  e On the contrary / In fact
  f On the contrary / In fact
  g Unfortunately
3 *Possible answers:*
  a … she works very hard.
  b … she turned him down.
  c … a landrover came by and pulled them back into town.
  d … the work's very interesting.
  e … it was closed while I was there.

Unit 21 Finding out

A Questions

2 What (sort/kind of clothes) shall I wear?
3 How long did it take you to find the house?
4 What kind/sort/brand of toothpaste do you use?
5 How often do they visit the States?
6 How much (money) did you have with you?
7 What flavour chewing gum do you like best?
8 How far is your flat from the centre? / How far from the centre is your flat?

B They don't know …

They don't know what he was typing when he died.
They don't know how the murderer knew that he would be there.
They don't know what the murderer hit him with.
They don't know if/whether Sir Hugh knew the murderer (or not).
They don't know where the murderer has hidden the murder weapon.
They don't know if/whether the murderer is still in the house (or not).
They don't know who killed Sir Hugh.

C Reported questions

2 … if/whether she would pick him up from the office after work.
3 … how long he had been waiting.
4 … when he/she would be back from lunch.
5 … how much he had in his account.
6 … if/whether he had cleaned his teeth.
7 … if/whether he could have the day off on Friday.
8 … when the world was going to end.

D Question tags

1 El Greco wasn't Greek, was he?
2 You haven't met the Prime Minister, have you?
3 He was arrested for shoplifting, wasn't he?
4 He's a bit strange, isn't he?
5 She's always losing her handbag, isn't she?
6 Ostriches can't fly, can they?
7 You won't tell anyone, will you?

Listening: Phone conversation

1 – Someone in a computer repair shop.
  – Her printer, which isn't working.
  – The motor has burnt out.
2 *See tapescript.*

Pronunciation: Changing tones

2 *a* He's studying French ↘ at university. ↗
  b He's studying French ↘ at university. ↘
  c No. We got married ↘ on Saturday. ↘
  d No. I stayed at home ↘ last night. ↗
  e Oh, I see him ↗ almost every day. ↘

Reading: A bit of luck

1 *a* In a station bookstall.
  b That he didn't know anything about her.
2 – He realises she must have come from the west side of the station, so he can find out what buses would take her there.
  – He saw the *Nursing Journal*, and realised she was a nurse.
  – She hadn't had coffee since 4 (a.m.) – so she'd been on night duty.
  – He finds Zena Yates in the hospital, and through her finds the woman.
3 Something like 'Have you lent a suitcase to anyone recently?'
4 Valeria Watson

Unit 22 Speaking personally

A Three ways of talking about feelings

1
depress	depressed	*depressing*
embarrass	*embarrassed*	embarrassing
excite	*excited*	*exciting*
frighten	frightened	*frightening*
relax	*relaxed*	*relaxing*
upset	*upset*	upsetting
worry	*worried*	*worrying*

2 *b* embarrassing   *g* upset
  c frightened   *h* embarrassed
  d depressed   *i* worry
  e relax   *j* relaxing
  f frightens (worries); exciting

C Good and bad

1 brilliant; terrific; wonderful
2 awful; dreadful; terrible
3 *a* boring   *c* exciting
  b amusing, entertaining   *d* disappointing
4 fascinating

Listening: James Bond films

2 *a* 2, 3 *c* 3 *e* 2 *g* 1
  b 2 *d* 3 *f* 1
3 *a* I've grown out of them.
    The gadgets … seem ridiculous to our generation.
  b pure escapism
    you can switch off
  c (it had) brilliant theme music
    they followed the books pretty closely

Phrasal verbs: Three-word verbs (2)

1 *a* put up with   *d* look up to
  b look out on   *e* look down on
  c get down to   *f* stand up for
3 *a* looks up to   *d* looks out on
  b got down to   *e* put up with
  c looks down on   *f* stood up for

Writing skills: Sequence: unexpected events

1 Normal sequence of events: *1a, 2a, 3a*.
  Something sudden and unexpected: *1b, 2b, 3b*.
2 *Possible answers:*
  a He was just about to drink the wine …
  b After the waiter brought her the change …
  c I was just getting on the bus …
  d He'd just put the cake in the oven …
  e Before I went into the flat …
3 *Possible anwer:*
I'd just come home when the telephone rang. A voice said, 'Meet me downstairs in ten minutes – it's important.' I put my coat on, and I was just going out of the door when the phone rang again. The same voice said, 'Walk straight across the street to the other side.' While I was crossing the street, I heard the sound of a car accelerating. I ran as fast as I could and I'd just reached the pavement when a Mercedes drove past, missing me by inches.

Unit 23 The unreal past

A What would you have done?

Possible answers:
1 I wouldn't have carried on reading my paper.
  I would have complained / walked out.
2 I would have told him to stop it.
  I would have sent him out of the room.
3 I would have waited for her.
  I would have helped her with her suitcases.
4 I would have tried to suck out the poison.
  I would have walked slowly – I wouldn't have run.

B Third conditionals

Possible answers:
1 … if I had had enough money.
2 … I wouldn't have offered them lamb curry.
3 If that woman hadn't shouted …
4 … if you hadn't left it on the pavement.
5 … it wouldn't have bitten you.
6 If he'd said that to me …
7 … if they'd had some better music.

C It's all your fault

Possible answers:
1 If you'd got here sooner …
2 If you'd packed some blankets, we wouldn't be so cold.
  If you'd filled up with petrol, we'd be home by now.
3 If you'd worn a mask, we wouldn't be in prison.
  If you hadn't dropped the money, we'd be having the time of our lives in Las Vegas.
4 If you'd brought the right equipment, we wouldn't be lying here covered in bandages.
  If you'd been more careful, we'd be on the top of the mountain watching the sun go down.

D It's all my own fault

Possible answers:
2 I wish I'd brought some warm clothes.
  I should have filled up with petrol.
  I wish we'd stayed at home.
3 I wish we'd never robbed the bank.
  We should have planned it more carefully.
  I wish we'd managed to get to Las Vegas.
4 We should have taken the proper equipment.
  I wish we'd chosen an easier mountain.
  I shouldn't have been so careless.

Listening: A better place

1 We should *listen* to *other people*.
  We should get our power from *water* instead of *oil*.
  Men should have *babies*.
  Cars produce *exhaust* fumes.
  Guns cause a huge number of *injuries*.
2 1*a*; 2*b*; 3*b*; 4*b*; 5*a*

Reading: If things had been different …

a False   *f* False   *j* True
b False   *g* True   *k* False
c False   *h* False   *l* False
d Can't tell   *i* True   *m* Can't tell
e True

Unit 24 Life on Earth

A Environment quiz

1 global   5 nuclear   9 Sahara
2 rain   6 chemicals   10 forest
3 ozone   7 carbon   11 greenhouse
4 power   8 pollution

Listening: How green are you?

1	1	2	3
buy 'green' products	✔	?	✔
don't waste paper	✗	✔	✔
don't waste plastic	✗	?	✔
avoid car travel	✗	✗	✔
recycle glass/paper	?	✔	✔
Possible score	2–3	4–6	7–9

2 1 She doesn't buy products if they've got CFC gases.
    She doesn't take her own bag shopping; she keeps getting new ones from shops.

2 He doesn't run the tap while he's cleaning his teeth.
  He turns the heating up rather than put on a jumper.
3 All the waste paper is collected and recycled.
  She doesn't recycle cans – just throws them away.

Phrasal verbs: Review

1 *a* … on our journey.   *e* … from the station.
  b … to my homework.   *f* … on a large lake.
  c … the answer.   *g* … some new clothes.
  d … their baby.   *h* … an old friend.
2 *a* … let me down.   *e* … give them away.
  b … took off.   *f* … do without her.
  c … deal with them.   *g* … put up with her/it?
  d … catch up with them.   *h* … gets over it soon.

Writing skills: Organising ideas

1 They show more clearly how the second and third sentences are connected to the first. They make it clear that the writer is talking about an *advantage* of word-processors, and about *reasons* for the disappearance of frogs and toads.
2 *Possible answers:*
  a The (only) result will be that even more people will travel by car …
  b The (main) reason was that the Indians …
  c The problem is that they need at least …
  d The only problem is that it uses up …
  e The main advantage is that I can work …
3 *Possible continuations:*
  a A better solution would be to improve bus services and build an underground railway.
  b Another reason was that the white settlers had better weapons and a more organised army.
  c They can also be very noisy, which is very annoying for the neighbours.
  d Also, I often get stopped by the police, and have to pay fines for speeding.
  e If I feel like it, I can take a week off work, or I can decide to work over the weekend.

Review Units 19–24

1 Sentence rewriting

1 I've had this typewriter since I left school.
2 They've been watching TV for four hours.
3 It's 500 years since the volcano (last) erupted.
4 I've no idea where she lives.
5 He asked me whether I'd locked the front door.
6 If I'd had enough money, I would have bought it.
7 I wish I'd apologised.

2 Asking questions

1 How long have you been learning Chinese?
2 You haven't seen my glasses, have you?
3 What flavour (ice-cream) would you like?
4 What make of car have you got / do you have / do you drive?
5 How long does it take to get there by bus?
6 Could you tell me the way to the station / how to get to the station / where the station is?
7 Penguins live at the North Pole, don't they?

3 Vocabulary

1 *Birth:* christen, midwife
  Marriage: bridegroom, honeymoon, reception
  Death: cemetery, coffin, funeral, mourning
2 ambitious – wants to be Prime Minister
  naughty – behaves like a child
  self-conscious – gets embarrassed easily
  rebellious – dislikes authority
  wise – knows a lot about life
3 *Possible answers:*
  a worried   *c* depressed
  b relaxed   *d* excited
4 entertaining – amusing
  dull – boring
  terrible – dreadful
  terrific – brilliant
  interesting – fascinating
5 *a* Acid   *d* rainforests; extinct
  b layer   *e* power
  c greenhouse; global

4 Fill the gaps

1 allowed; fight/die; enough; law
2 was; when; how; been; for; would; refused; get; off/away
3 hit; have; become; human; much/far; than

6 Dictation

I saw a fantastic horror film last night. It was all about a village where strange creatures were attacking young people at night and carrying them off. No-one knew what they were, or why they were doing it. But the attacks always happened near the cemetery, and people started to believe that the creatures were dead bodies which were coming out of their graves.

    Anyway, one girl managed to get away when she was attacked, and she said she thought the creature had recognised her and let her go.

    And in the end it turned out that the creature was her grandfather, who lived in an old people's home near the church. This mad doctor who ran the home had discovered a way to make old people young again, using blood taken from teenagers, and he was giving these elderly people an amazing drug which temporarily turned them into monsters, and was sending them out at night to catch teenagers for his experiments. But when the old man saw his granddaughter, he realised what was happening, and told the others. And they attacked the mad scientist and killed him. It was really enjoyable.

Phrasal verbs: reference

Introduction

Phrasal verbs have two parts: a *verb* (e.g. *make, go, get*) and a *'small word'* (e.g. *on, up, out, with*). This 'small word' may be an adverb or a preposition. Some phrasal verbs (Type 4, below) have two 'small words'.

Types of phrasal verb

Type 1: *Verb + adverb* (Units 4, 6)

take off	The plane *took off*.
get up	I *get up* at 6 o'clock.

These verbs are intransitive (they have no object).

Type 2: *Verb + noun + adverb* (Units 8, 10, 12, 14)

take ... off	He *took* his shoes *off*.
give ... away	She *gave* all her money *away*.

These verbs are transitive (they have an object: *shoes, money*).

If the object is a noun, the adverb can come *before* or *after* it. So we can say:

He *took* his shoes *off*. or
He *took off* his shoes.

If the object is a pronoun (*him, her, it, them*), the adverb must come *after* it. So we can say:

He *took* them *off*.   but not ~~He took off them.~~

Type 3: *Verb + preposition + noun* (Units 16, 18)

look for	I'm *looking for* my glasses.
take after	She *takes after* her mother.

These are sometimes called 'prepositional verbs'. The preposition (*for, after,* etc.) must come *before* the noun. (We cannot say ~~I'm looking my glasses for.~~)

Type 4: *Verb + adverb + preposition + noun* (Units 20, 22)

run out of	I've *run out of* matches.
get down to	It's time to *get down to* some work.

These are sometimes called 'three-word verbs'. They are a combination of Types 1 and 3.

The meanings of phrasal verbs

With some phrasal verbs, the meaning is obvious:

He *got in* the car and *drove off*.
He *turned round* and saw me.

But many phrasal verbs have an 'idiomatic' meaning which cannot easily be guessed from the individual words:

They *turned up* an hour later (= arrived).
She *made* the story *up* (= invented).
I'm trying to *cut down on* cigarettes (= smoke less).

Some common 'idiomatic' phrasal verbs with their meanings

Type 1

carry on	=	continue
find out	=	discover
grow up	=	become adult
set off	=	start (a journey)
settle down	=	live in one place
take off	=	leave the ground
turn up	=	arrive (unexpectedly)

Type 2

bring sg. up	=	introduce (a topic)
bring s.o. up	=	raise (a child)
give sg. away	=	reveal (a secret); give (for no money)
give sg. up	=	stop (doing)
let s.o. down	=	disappoint
look sg. up	=	find the meaning (of a word)
look s.o. up	=	visit (after a long time)
make sg./s.o. out	=	understand
make sg. up	=	invent
pick sg. up	=	take (from the ground)
pick s.o. up	=	collect, meet
put s.o. down	=	criticise/humiliate
put sg. off	=	delay, postpone
put sg. up	=	build, construct
put s.o. up	=	have to stay (as a guest)
ring s.o. up	=	telephone
run sg./s.o. over	=	drive over (in a car)
take sg. up	=	start (doing)
talk s.o. round	=	persuade
think sg. over	=	consider carefully
turn s.o./sg. down	=	refuse
turn sg. up/down	=	make louder/quieter
work sg. out	=	find the answer (to a problem)

Type 3

call for sg./s.o.	=	collect
come across sg.	=	find (by chance)
cope with sg.	=	manage
deal with sg.	=	be concerned with
(could) do with sg.	=	would like
(can't) do without sg./s.o.	=	need
get over sg.	=	recover from
go off sg./s.o.	=	stop liking
look after sg./s.o.	=	care for, be responsible for
look into sg.	=	investigate
run into s.o.	=	meet (by chance)
take after s.o.	=	resemble (an older relative)
take to sg./s.o.	=	like, be attracted to

Type 4

catch up with sg./s.o.	=	draw level with
cut down on sg.	=	reduce the amount of
get down to sg.	=	start doing
get on with sg.	=	make progress with, continue
get on with s.o.	=	like being with
look down on s.o.	=	despise
look out for sg./s.o.	=	watch for, be careful of
look out on sg.	=	have a view of
look up to s.o.	=	respect
put up with sg./s.o.	=	tolerate
run out of sg.	=	have no more of
stand up for sg./s.o.	=	defend

sg.= something   s.o.= someone